Parties, Power and Policy-making

This book explains the conditions under which political parties in government were able to influence economic growth in post-communist European countries. It highlights higher education and international investment as the two essentially related areas that have been steered by governments.

The book illustrates how these countries have become reliant on multinational companies (MNCs), given their governments' strategy to attract foreign capital, how political and economic factors are intertwined and how political parties in power can have a strong influence on the growth prospects of these economies. Furthermore, it illuminates the extent to which political parties use their space for manoeuvres when enacting policies and how they respond to their constituencies when doing so. It shows how structural conditions such as the dependence on MNCs influence policies, and how this pattern varies across Central and Eastern Europe. The book brings political parties back into the discussion on political economy and back into the analyses of welfare politics, varieties of capitalism, and democratic capitalism.

This text will be of key interest to scholars and students of comparative politics and comparative political economy, European policy-making, Central and Eastern Europe, trade, welfare and development, and higher education.

Silvana Tarlea is a post-doctoral researcher at the Institute for European Global Studies and in the Political Science Department at the University of Basel in Switzerland. She obtained her doctorate from the University of Oxford, Nuffield College.

Routledge/UACES Contemporary European Studies

Edited by Chad Damro, University of Edinburgh, UK, Elaine Fahey, City University London, UK, and David Howarth, University of Luxembourg, Luxembourg, on behalf of the University Association for Contemporary European Studies.

The primary objective of the new Contemporary European Studies series is to provide a research outlet for scholars of European Studies from all disciplines. The series publishes important scholarly works and aims to forge for itself an international reputation.

Parties, Power and Policy-making
From Higher Education to Multinationals in Post-Communist Societies
Silvana Tarlea

Competitiveness and Solidarity in the European Union
Interdisciplinary Perspectives
Edited by Paolo Chiocchetti and Frédéric Allemand

Changing Borders in Europe
Exploring the Dynamics of Integration, Differentiation and Self-Determination in the European Union
Edited by Jacint Jordana, Michael Keating, Axel Marx and Jan Wouters

Citizenship, Nation-building and Identity in the EU
The Contribution of Erasmus Student Mobility
Cherry James

UACES

Parties, Power and Policy-making

From Higher Education to Multinationals in Post-Communist Societies

Silvana Tarlea

Routledge
Taylor & Francis Group
LONDON AND NEW YORK

UACES

First published 2019 by Routledge
2 Park Square, Milton Park, Abingdon, Oxon OX14 4RN
52 Vanderbilt Avenue, New York, NY 10017

First issued in paperback 2020

Routledge is an imprint of the Taylor & Francis Group, an informa business

British Library Cataloguing in Publication Data
A catalogue record for this book is available from the British Library

Library of Congress Cataloging-in-Publication Data
A catalog record has been requested for this book

ISBN 13: 978-0-367-66321-6 (pbk)
ISBN 13: 978-1-138-04723-5 (hbk)

Typeset in Times New Roman
by Taylor & Francis Books

Contents

Illustrations

Figures

Tables

Acknowledgements

This book has benefitted from the generous support and advice of many people throughout the years. It has developed from the DPhil thesis that I wrote at the University of Oxford, Nuffield College. I was guided by David Soskice whom I would like to thank for his generous support. He gracefully shaped my thinking while teaching me to stand on my feet. His disagreements were always kind but firm. *This is excellent work, but now let's forget about it* was just one way in which he'd argue differently. And when it seemed like the end was nowhere in sight, he knew how to make it more manageable. Having him on my side is such a privilege.

Gwendolyn Sasse at Nuffield has been much more than a college advisor. She is a role model who has made it all seem less intimidating despite being so intimidatingly successful herself. She was kind and crisp at difficult stages of the research. Bob Hancké and Ben Ansell provided critical feedback at various stages for which I am very thankful.

Earlier on, while a graduate student in Amsterdam, I was fortunate to be guided by Annette Freyberg-Inan. She taught me how to write and how to embrace analytical thinking. At the University of Bucharest, where I was an undergraduate student, Cristian Preda, Silvia Marton and Catalin Avramescu were highly inspiring. Their intellectual rigor, the dedication to their students and to their profession have been a guiding light for me and for many of their students.

At the European University Institute, Laszlo Bruszt, Doro Bohle and Bela Greskovits have known the project in its various stages and have been warm and helpful. Their knowledge of the region and their curiosity continue to inspire me. Much of this book has been presented at conferences and seminars where I received much useful feedback. I would like to especially thank Marius Busemeyer. Many others offered their time and support, I am sure that I am forgetting many.

In Basel, I have found a prolific environment for research and I could not have wished for a better place. Stefanie Bailer and Ralph Weber have given me the opportunity of working with them and of becoming part of a growing department. I am very thankful for these exciting times.

I would also like to thank friends and family. Nehal Davison at Oxford and later on in many places in the world has been a wonderful friend who has made navigating British society and life in general more enjoyable. Dingeman Wiertz has been a great friend. I have been fortunate to meet them both. And the many friends in every place where I lived – I stopped counting after the fifth move – they all know who they are, thanks.

And last but not least, my family. My parents, Rodica and Ioan, have been there whenever things got difficult. It has not been clear where this was going to lead, but they trusted me without asking anything in return. I hope to be such a parent for our sons as well. My parents-in-law, Virginia and Alin, have been there for us whenever the road got bumpier. And it did. My sister, Brindusa, for being the kindest person on earth.

I am so pleased to see my first book coming to light. And none of this would have been possible without Filip.

Basel
July 19, 2018

Introduction

> Optimism was justifiable. The removal of the overwhelming apparatus of political control over economic activity could only mean prosperity in the medium term. The Central and Eastern European and former Soviet Union countries were well prepared for rapid take-off: they were industrialized, they had reasonably educated and healthy labor forces, and population growth was minimal. Technology was lagging, but with the free flow of information and Western assistance, that could be overcome. Moreover, there was substantial technical progress in the defense sector that, maybe, could spill over the economy, reinforcing optimistic predictions. Some countries (notably Poland) had to tackle macroeconomic imbalances first, but for that economists felt well equipped. Prosperity was, finally, around the corner.
>
> (Campos and Coricelli 2002: 1)

Introduction

In 1989, eight out of 100 students finishing high school in Romania were going to university. By 2010, this number had risen to 60, due to a steady enrolment increase during the entire period.[1] One would expect this story to be matched by an equivalently extraordinary economic growth trend. However, Romania still registers one of the lowest GDPs in the region, despite having had the most impressive boom in higher education (HE).[2] This picture fits many of the former communist countries that have now become members of the European Union.[3] Most of these registered in 2010 enrolments that had more than doubled since 1989 (UNESCO 2014).[4] But they have recorded more modest economic growth than initially envisaged by optimistic views of economic transformation as summarized by Campos and Coricelli (2002) in the beginning paragraph of this chapter. In contrast to Romania, other countries of the region have been more successful. Having witnessed an equally impressive increase in HE enrolment, Estonia's economy has boomed during this time, having become a textbook example for economic governance around the world (Panagiotou 2001). While many factors shape economic success, good governance being one of them, the cases of Romania and that of Estonia show that the changes in HE enrolment have been associated with economic growth in some countries but less in others.

The limited economic success is well captured by recent Global Competitiveness Reports (World Economic Forum 2013), in which the two newest members of the European Union, Bulgaria and Romania, are listed as undergoing a second stage of development. However, Poland and Hungary are part of the group of intermediary economies, while Slovenia, Estonia and the Czech Republic have joined the group of advanced, innovation-driven economies, in their third level of development. Even accounting for the slightly different initial starting conditions and for the complex structures determining economic success, the countries have diverged after the fall of communism. Thus, this book unpacks the conditions under which some countries upgrade economically while others do not by highlighting the crucial role of human capital for this process. Despite broadly similar political economic histories these countries have diverged from one another and most importantly from the rest of the European Union to which they now belong. What are the factors that best explain these developments? The book argues that these diverging economic growth trends are closely related to the variation in HE evolution.

Most of the Central and Eastern Europe (CEE) countries have surpassed the UK or Germany in terms of HE enrolment. Gross enrolment levels in the UK reached 60 per cent in 2010. The impressive trends in HE might seem less surprising given their extraordinary context: CEE countries have registered fundamental structural changes, moving during this time-frame from centrally planned and autarkic economies to free and open market economies. Simultaneously, they have embarked on a democratization process that allowed for a shift from an authoritarian regime to a by-now functional democratic one. Hence, the revolutionary shift in HE provision fits the overall picture of structural changes taking place in these countries. During this process, differences between countries have sharpened while the overall region has witnessed increasing levels of education accompanied by a relatively low (but increasing) level of economic growth. Differences in economic performance between the countries of the region have existed already before the fall of the Berlin wall, but these have increased since 1989. But what justifies the inquiry of this book is that; absolute inequality between the Eastern and the Western European (WE) countries has increased since 1989 (See Figure 0.1, which contrasts Western European Countries (EU 18) to the new EU members (CEE 10)).

Prominent work suggests that an increase in the level of skills in an economy is linked to economic growth at the individual and macro level (Goldin and Katz 2009). Research in economics (Glaeser 2011; Lindahl and Krueger 2001; Hanushek and Woessmann 2011), as well as advice from international organizations aimed at helping developing economies to grow, emphasizes the importance of skills for economic success. Hence, we would expect that this general upskilling would translate into growth in all countries of the region. Figure 0.1 shows that the economies of CEE have started catching up with the rest of Europe further to the north, west and south. Nevertheless, the nominal GDP/capita differences between these two sets of countries have increased from $15,000 in 1989 to $40,000 in 2010. At the same time, though, the ratios of their GDPs have increased from 16 to 27 per cent (CEE as compared with WE).[5] This data is discussed in more detail in Chapter 3.

These radical dynamics in HE in the region and the variation in economic growth and in economic sophistication between countries seem *puzzling*. Economic growth and economic sophistication are determined by a set of complex interactions, of which education is one important part. The book identifies a set of actors that co-determine the increasing enrolments and the difference in economic success in these countries. The explanation relies on a theoretical model defined in the varieties of capitalism (VoC) tradition. This is the dependent market economy (DME) model adeptly defined by Nölke and Vliegenthart (2009). Drawing from this model, it argues that multinational companies (MNCs) play an important role in these political economies. The novel argument of this book is that it links this model to the dynamics in HE. Furthermore, political parties in government have also steered HE by almost unilaterally liberalizing enrolment while at the same time making divergent decisions regarding spending for HE. The interplay between MNCs, HE institutions and political parties in government determines *how skills are used* and this is in turn linked to economic success. An increasing HE enrolment will lead to economic upgrading only if employers demand sophisticated skills.

This introduction proceeds as follows: it first provides a brief overview of the political-economic processes in the region that it aims to explain, it then engages with the relevance of this research and its contribution to ongoing scholarly debates while presenting the state of the art in the discipline. It then

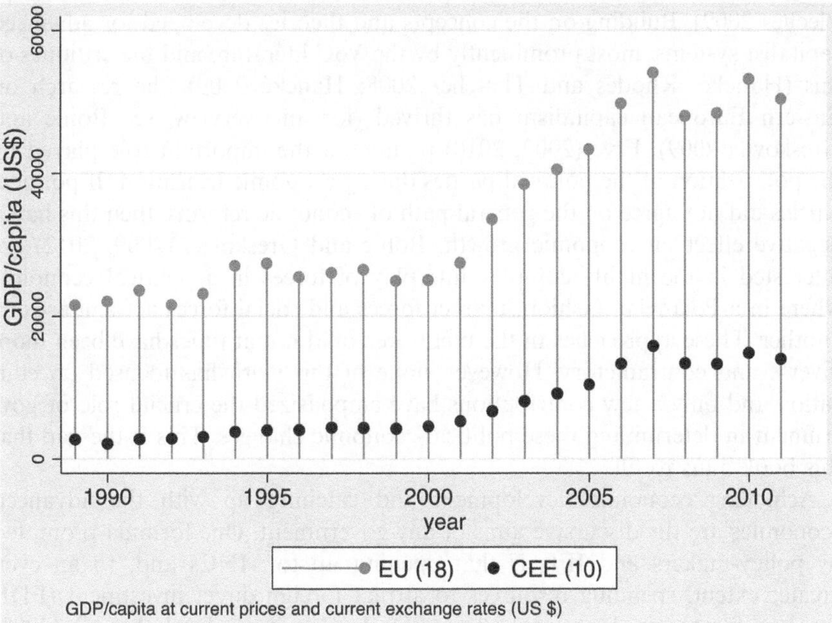

Figure 0.1 GDP/capita over time

explains the methodological foundations, continuing with an overview of each chapter the book, before concluding.

1 Motivation

The high expectations at the beginning of the 1990s that the economies of CEE would develop quickly and join the group of advanced, knowledge-based economies are by and large still to be met, as well captured by Campos and Coricelli (2002), quoted in the opening paragraph of this chapter. Embracing a new way to organize their economies and polities has not brought equal success to these countries. Surprisingly enough, these expectations have remained largely unfulfilled even during the "golden years" preceding the global economic crisis that started in 2008, when economic growth rates were positive (see Figure 0.1). Some of these countries seem to have learnt that embracing the rules of the free market economy game, which were zealously promoted by the Western democratic countries and by international financial institutions (IFI), especially in the 1990s (Drahokoupil 2008), is not only insufficient for becoming a successful export-oriented economy but also may hinder their long-term economic performance.

The reasons behind why some of these transition countries have been rather slow in catching up with their Western role-models, while others have been more successful, have prompted a number of studies in the growing literature on European political economy (e.g. Bandelj 2008; Bohle and Greskovits 2006, 2012; Cernat 2006; Drahokoupil 2009; Feldmann 2006; Frye 2010; Pop-Eleches 2009). Building on the concepts and theories developed for advanced capitalist systems, most prominently by the VoC literature and the critiques of this (Hancké, Rhodes and Thatcher 2008; Hancké 2009), the research on Eastern European capitalism has thrived (for an overview, see Bohle and Greskovits 2009). Frye (2002, 2010) points out the important role played by the polarization of the political parties during economic transition. If political parties did not agree on the general path of economic reforms, then this had a negative effect on economic growth. Bohle and Greskovits (2009, 2012) are interested in the highly complex interplay of forces in a political economy, where in a Polanyian fashion, market forces and social forces act against one another. These approaches in the literature could not at times have been more diverse and contradictory. However, none of this work has focused on education and only a few contributions have emphasized the crucial role of government in determining these political-economic changes. This is the gap that this book aims to fill.

Achieving economic development and catching up with the advanced economies are the discursive aims of any government. One formula promoted by policy-makers and IFIs is that opening up to MNCs and, to an even greater extent, spending resources to attract foreign direct investment (FDI) are key factors in long-term economic development. Drahokoupil (2009) provides a thorough overview of the role of IFIs in CEE, while Pop-Eleches

(2009) discusses their role during crises. While this scenario seems to have played out for some countries (such as Slovenia and the Czech Republic), and for certain sectors in a few economies (i.e. the automobile industry in Slovakia and Hungary or the IT and services sector in Poland), many of these countries have not managed to reach sustainable economic growth through this strategy. At the same time, increased levels of education have been shown to lead to economic growth (Hanushek and Woessmann 2011).

CEE is a suitable region for studying the relationship between employers – particularly MNCs – and institutions of skill formation and their politicization. These countries are relatively homogenous and thus comparable. First, the region shares a largely common political economic history: a relatively prosperous and democratic interwar period, followed by the communist experience after WWII and by democratization and marketization after 1989. Second, the countries have opened up to foreign capital relatively simultaneously after 1989. These CEE economies are more internationalized than most other developed economies as of 2012, being more dependent on foreign capital than any country in Europe, except for Luxembourg. Detailed data on this is presented in Chapter 2. Therefore, a compelling motivation to study the association of foreign capital and human capital formation in CEE is the heavy dependence on foreign capital of these economies. Hyperbolically, they can be considered the most suitable environment to study what awaits the rest of the world over the long run.[6] Third, both the democratization and the marketization processes have been largely supported by international organizations and by WE governments relatively simultaneously. Thus, this simultaneous outside influence on all CEE countries can be (at least partially) discounted in the comparative analysis of these countries. Fourth, the CEE countries have all been part of a Europeanization process (Schimmelfennig and Sedelmeier 2005), including membership to the European Union, which deeply influenced the processes in HE. Fifth, education policies during communism and in the post-communist period have been largely similar (Scott 2002). Sixth, while the previous five factors point to broad similarities between countries, there has been great variation in HE outcomes and economic sophistication. The book tackles this variation.

Analyzing the links between MNCs, HE institutions and political parties is a complex endeavour. Hence, several types of analyses are used in the book, linking the corners of this triangle. The unit of analysis shifts from the region, to the country and further to the firm and individual political party. First, trends characterizing the entire CEE region are considered. Second, the book identifies the sources of variation in the HE policies between countries. Cases are chosen from within a region for comparability reasons, but the processes considered are generalizable outside the region. The lessons drawn from these studies are relevant beyond the geographical and historical boundaries covered empirically. Third, individual-level analyses are conducted as well, focusing on political parties and on individual firms. At the same time, this book fills an intellectual void on the political economic determinants of education policies in CEE.

2 Theoretical foundations

This research draws on diverse intellectual traditions and this diversity stems from at least two sources. First, the explanation advanced here accounts for a variety of institutions, such as institutions of skill formation, partisan politics as well as the rich literature on MNCs. Therefore, we engage the debates surrounding research on these institutions. Second, the theoretical and the methodological debates in comparative political economy have intensified over the years, which underlines the importance of a methodologically sound approach. Drawing on diverse types of work that are at times fundamentally critical of one another, this contribution aims to reconcile apparently antagonistic theoretical traditions, explained in more detail in the following sections.

2.1 Skill formation in comparative political economy

This book contributes to the literature on institutional political economy, as broadly defined. It builds critically on the VoC literature. In its initial formulation, this theory argued that we can distinguish between two different forms of capitalism: the liberal (LME) and the coordinated market economy (CME) (Hall and Soskice 2001). These two varieties have comparative advantages in the world economy: the CME is prone to be a hub of incremental innovation, while the LME, of radical innovation. By putting the firm at the centre of analysis, this tradition argues that different coordination mechanisms characterize each type of capitalism. Interestingly, by analyzing how firms act in relation to important institutional actors one can derive an understanding of how these political-economic systems work as a whole – this is understood almost ontologically. Differences between these two forms of capitalism are established early on, already at the level of the education system – the focus in this literature is usually on vocational training. These political-economic systems evolve differently depending on these early-established differences. Two main insights are drawn from this approach, which are further explored: the relevance of firms and their relation to education. However, given the specificities of CEE political economies, a VoC approach leads us to consider specific forms of these institutions: MNCs rather than domestic ones, given the structural power of MNCs in the region (Eurostat 2014). Similarly, instead of focusing on vocational training, the emphasis lies on HE, given its structural relevance in these new political economies.

Skill formation is slowly capturing more of the attention of political economists and is a building block of this research and, in essence, of the VoC approach. The main argument of scholars of skill formation is that the way in which firms and individuals adapt to their environment is determined and, at the same time, consequential for their training decisions for their individual investments in education and for their preferences towards the welfare state or redistribution (see, for example, Iversen and Soskice 2001). This is important in itself as the incentives of individuals to invest in skills will, on the long run, be consequential for economic growth as well. Moreover, these individual incentives could be translated into policy through the representation of these interests in government. This emphasizes the importance of the electoral determinants of human capital formation. However, most existing literature focuses on developed economies (Ansell [2010] also considers the rest of the world). This book should begin to fill the gap by focusing on CEE countries as an example of upper-middle-income economies. Moreover, "the varieties of capitalism debate provides an appropriate access route to studying these complementarities between education, welfare states and political institutions" (Busemeyer and Trampusch 2011: 434; see also Powell and Trampusch 2012).

This line of research considers institutions of skill formation to be complementary, which has been a legitimate target of criticism of the VoC literature (Crouch et al. 2005). Therefore, the theoretical approach of book is agnostic about the nature of the links between the institutions discussed – HE, MNCs, governments. Nonetheless, the empirics have revealed that the changes that have taken place in the different policy areas did not take place in a vacuum. Rather, they co-evolved, which is a sign of institutional coupling. While analyzing the HE market in Romania presented in detail in Chapter 2, we found that at the same time as the education market was liberalizing, state-owned enterprises were being privatized. Put differently, we should not be surprised that the education market became highly liberalized, when similar dynamics were taking place in other sectors of the economy, such as the privatization of state-owned enterprises. No matter how simple this argument, it is a surprisingly new contribution to the scholarly work in the field. Pointing towards this co-evolution is another contribution of this book.

Moreover, complementarity tends in the VoC literature to have some positive connotations. As this book argues extensively, these complementarities can also be negative, with different institutions dragging one another down as is the case in the Romanian DME, which is characterized by a low-skills equilibrium. This research also considers the possibility that some complementarities are not self-reinforcing or that certain elements in the system do not reinforce one another and may even be contradictory. Moreover, these dynamics are not always linear. The case of the Orbán government after 2010 in Hungary clearly shows that the support of political parties for investments in the economy cannot be taken for granted (Bayer 2018). The empirical chapters provide more details on this front.

Going further, an appropriate criticism of certain formulations of the VoC literature is that it is functionalist. Pierson (2004) provides an excellent and intuitive discussion of functionalist theories more generally by arguing that explaining the emergence of institutional arrangements through their envisaged consequences is problematic. He is wary of the sizable time lag between actor's actions and the long-term consequences of those actions. Thus, the long-term effects of institutional choices, which are frequently the most profound and interesting ones, should often be seen as the by-products of social processes rather than embodying the goals of social actors (Pierson 2004: 14).

The book pays close attention to the important differences between *anticipated* effects and *actual* effects.

2.2 Dependency theory in Eastern Europe and Latin America

The way in which the concept of the DME is used and redefined here could perhaps be misleading and requires some clarification. Dependency stems from reliance on capital from abroad through MNCs and the inability (or very limited ability) of the domestic sector to further capitalize on this foreign capital. This argument builds on the initial formulation of the dependency theory: "From the economic point of view a system is dependent when the accumulation and expansion of capital cannot find its essential dynamic component inside the system" (Cardoso and Faletto 1979: XX). The exodus of high-skilled individuals from the economy reinforces this dependency. However, it is not *the degree of dependency* that is relevant for the economic setup (and so for our model), but rather *the effect this dependency* has on the sophistication level of the domestic market more generally. Here, several explanations are needed. Nölke and Vliegenthart (2009) point out that dependency determines the average level of economic sophistication. Nevertheless, they do not provide thorough causal explanations of the ways in which individual incentives are determined by this dependency. The effects of this dependency are more profound and far-reaching than simply determining the types of goods and services that are produced. This is further disentangled in the empirical chapters.

The high reliance on foreign capital should not come as a surprise given the many interdependencies that exist between the domestic economies of advanced capitalist countries. They too are dependent on MNCs, on IFIs, on cross-border migration or on the supply of and demand for goods and services that originate outside their own markets. However, these transnational exchanges of goods and services do not seem to systematically weaken either of the markets involved, or to keep one of them at a low level of sophistication, because this is a mutual exchange, an *interdependency.* Therefore, the argument for the prevalence of the DME model in CEE does not rest on the fact that a Central or Eastern European economy has more MNCs than other European economies, but that *the effect* of MNCs on these DMEs is rather one-sided.

One stream of literature that relates to the DME model, at least as far as the terminology is concerned, emerged in the 1970s, the dependency school. This literature questions the positive effects of MNCs in developing countries (Cardoso and Faletto 1979; Evans 1979). Bohle and Greskovits (2012) rely on this literature when correctly criticizing the DME model as formulated by

Nölke and Vliegenthart (2009) for not accounting for the lasting scarcity of human capital, which was the case in Latin America. This contribution seeks to account for this weakness. Moreover, the DME model does not imply by default a world order in the Wallerstein (1974) tradition, divided between core and periphery, in which the DME countries represent a (semi-) periphery. Some versions of the DME model may allow for an interpretation consistent with this worldview. However, scholars are due to provide more nuanced interpretations today than it was possible in the 1970s. One such source of variation in these political economic systems is represented by the agency of political parties.

2.3 European approaches to political economy

Some of the contradictory approaches to the CEE political economies identify the initial types of CME and LME proposed by Hall and Soskice (2001), while others suggest new ones founded on diverse considerations. In a study of CEE capitalism, Mykhnenko (2007) concludes that CEE countries show combined features of both CMEs and LMEs. Similarly, Buchen (2007) finds resemblances to both the LME and the CME types.

At the same time, relevant work has pictured a more nuanced role of foreign investors in CEE focusing on labour and industrial relations. Hancké (2011) identifies conditions under which MNCs contribute to the production of collective goods, especially through cooperation facilitated by chambers of commerce. In those circumstances, MNCs also contribute substantially to improving the industrial infrastructure. Bluhm (2001), in an analysis of German small and large firms in the Czech Republic and Poland, finds that firms do a selective transfer of vocational training programs in the country of destination.

Cernat (2006) builds on the classification system proposed by Rhodes and van Apeldoorn (1998), adding to the developmental types and coining, for Romania, the category of "cocktail capitalism". Political actors receive agency in this model (unlike in the initial VoC formulation), and Cernat stresses that it is not only the institutional choice of one model that matters but that the consistency of that choice determines the performance of economies. In a 2007 article, Bohle and Greskovits identified three distinct (non-LME/CME) transnational capitalisms in CEE: a neoliberal type in the Baltic States, an embedded neoliberal type in the Visegrad group and a neo-corporatist type in Slovenia. They build on a theoretical framework derived from Karl Polanyi's *Great Transformation* (1957), which is concerned with the fundamental conflict between market efficiency, social cohesion and political legitimacy. This approach overcomes some of the criticism that the initial VoC formulation has received, such as for its inability to explain institutional change. In this formulation, change occurs as a result of these conflicting forces in the market.

Each of these proposed models emphasizes different logics according to which these economies work and the different categories are embedded in diverse intellectual traditions. What seems to emerge from these diverging interpretations is that the existing theoretical framework has limited appeal for providing understanding of these transition economies. Furthermore, another important debate that needs to be accounted for is the Europeanization literature. This has contributed to explaining policy and institutional change in CEE by emphasizing the isomorphism in the region. Dobbins (2011) focuses on the Europeanization of HE, showing how institutions have evolved as a result of external pressure as well. Moreover, conditions imposed by the European Union for these countries' accession to the organization have been critical for institution-building (Hughes, Sasse and Gordon 2004; Schimmelfennig and Scholtz 2008). Political economists have left this area largely unaccounted for. This in turn enables and calls for further research to focus on exploring new frameworks that may have a closer fit with these economies.

In 2009, Nölke and Vliegenthart argued that it was the external dependency of the region that was the central characteristic of CEE. They propose a third basic variety (complementing the dichotomous framework of Hall and Soskice [2001]), a DME that captures the characteristics of the region. At the same time, Ben Schneider (2009) and Sanchez-Ancochea (2009) identified a hierarchical market economy (HME) in Latin America.

Put very schematically, DMEs show institutional complementarities between skilled but cheap labour, the transfer of technological innovations within transnational enterprises and the provision of capital via FDI. Given the central role of FDI, both investment and corporate governance are controlled by the MNCs. The local subsidiaries of these MNCs in CEE are financed internally within the company, and innovation within these MNCs is transmitted top-down within the hierarchies of the company. DMEs are used as assembly platforms for innovations made at headquarters. The subsidiaries of MNCs in developing markets will not be in favour of a generous public education system, or in favour of substantial investment by their company in innovation-relevant skills.

3 Contribution of this book to scholarly debates

The novelty of the approach of this book is that it focuses on the similarities between these new political economies: they have all inherited political-economic institutions specific to planned economies, the evolution of their HE systems has been largely similar, while all had little previously accumulated domestic capital. Whereas previous work has focused extensively on the divergences between these economies (prominent examples being Frye [2002] and Hancké [2011]), this contribution begins its study with the features that build a common denominator. The DME model proposed in this research is understood in a Weberian sense: it is an ideal model that simplifies complex socio-economic reality. Once having explained the specificities of a DME and how they characterize the countries of the region, the book moves on to explore differences between countries and their specific institutional configurations, trying to explain the determinants of the different outcomes.

3.1 Redefinition of the DME model

This book adds to a typology by developing a type, a variety of capitalism that it uses as an analytical tool, as proposed in the work of Collier, LaPorte and Seawright (2012). It adds to the ongoing debate about how to classify political economic modes of organization. It builds on a model of the economy: the DME model. One form of the DME model that is fully explored rests on a case study of Romania. Further, the book considers the variations on this model in order to explore its usefulness more generally. The important added value of developing a model within a typology lies in the fact that it brings order to complexity. Further, this model adds in two ways to the literature on VoC. First, it shows that the dichotomous framework offered by Hall and Soskice (2001) is limited in various ways, especially when intended to characterize CEE. It then builds critically on the third variety proposed by Nölke and Vliegenthart (2009), that of the DME. I argue that the DME model can be improved in at least three ways.

3.2 Role of political parties

First, the DME literature has paid no attention to politics. Nevertheless, we need to account for the role of governments in reinforcing the dependency of the economy and the ways in which it can contribute to breaking this vicious cycle. Political parties in government influence the HE system through mechanisms regulating enrolment and funding (Tarlea 2017; Tarlea and Freyberg-Inan 2018; Tarlea 2018). Governments played a key role at the beginning of the transition process by deciding to liberalize the HE market and to privatize state-owned companies. They continue to play a major role through the same financing and regulatory mechanisms. Moreover, as has been pointed out (Besley and Persson 2009; Iversen and Soskice 2009; Streeck 2009; Schmidt 2009), governments are an intrinsic actor in any political economy. With reference to CEE, we need to understand whether, and to what extent, the fall of the communist regimes has been disruptive to the ability of governments to foster economic development.

The book challenges existing wisdom about the role of political parties in shaping public policy in new democracies. Political parties have been largely neglected in political economy literature focusing on CEE (with the notable exception of Frye [2010]). Why do some governments spend more on HE than others? And what are the consequences of these decisions? The book engages the valuable work of Tavits (2009) and Grzymala-Busse (2007) in a larger framework and with a stronger emphasis on public policy and on the interaction between MNCs and governments.

3.3 Role of higher education

Second, the DME model has not yet developed an analysis of HE, of research or of training and its role in the production of economic growth (except for Tarlea and Freyberg-Inan 2018). Yet this is central if the DME model is to be vindicated. There is a wide agreement that the communist countries in Eastern Europe delivered good HE, especially in technical subjects. Nevertheless, they do not seem to have managed to preserve this advantage in the years since 1989. The book elaborates on the mechanisms that have accompanied the increase in enrolments in HE, while funding has lagged behind. This has led to a partial deterioration in the quality of HE. The empirical chapters provide an account of the possible explanatory factors and of their role in the overall economy.

Moreover, while in the VoC literature, attention is focused on vocational training; in the DME model, the HE system is the central element. This shift is motivated both theoretically and empirically. First, at the conceptual-theoretical level, the capacity of these economies to upgrade will depend on their ability to foster economic growth through services as well as through manufacturing industries that depend on the presence of marketable "high skills". These skills depend almost entirely on the supply of skills from universities. Hence, HE plays a similar structural role to that of vocational training in the classic VoC formulation by virtue of its potential to enable ecoBnomies to develop comparative advantages in the world economy. Second, at the empirical level, enrolment levels in vocational training in CEE have decreased significantly since the shift to a market economy was made, and vocational training has almost perished. Thirdly, and to some extent complementarily to the trends in vocational training, enrolment levels in HE institutions have increased considerably during the same period, in both absolute (number of degrees/years) and relative (gross enrolment ratios) terms.

3.4 Role of migration

The third contribution to the model highlights that the promising literature on the DME does not provide any analysis of migration, either emigration or immigration. Nevertheless, migration, both temporary and permanent, seems to greatly reinforce the dependency of these economies. Empirics suggest that, increasingly, the migration of highly skilled workers from the CEE countries depletes these economies from highly skilled workers. The movement – both in and out – of the highly skilled proportion of the population is important for the development of a country towards becoming one of what the World Economic Forum calls the *innovation-driven economies*, and that it must be included in any analysis of an economy (Docquier 2006, Sasse and Thielemann 2005). It seems that the trend of emigration by high-skilled individuals underpins the decline in the quality of HE. While there have been some studies of low-skilled emigration from Eastern Europe (e.g. Alexe 2011), we have limited knowledge about the dynamics of high-skilled individuals. Chapter 1, on Romania, argues that the trend of emigration by highly skilled individuals underpins the decline in the quality of HE.

The original insights of the DME are powerfully reinforced once these three factors are understood. This is where the research proposed in this book is heading. It aims at rounding up and strengthening the DME model. This is complemented by the (re-) introduction of the micro-foundations of the model and by a discussion of the origins of this DME model and institutional change within the model (particularly discussed in Chapter 4).

This book engages in a new research avenue in comparative political science, as it is only in recent years that scholars have started being more concerned with questions regarding the relevance of political variables in the development of education policies (Ansell [2010] and Busemeyer and Trampusch [2011] provide an excellent overview). Whether and how the composition and nature of governments matters for education and for upgrading of economic sophistication are questions that have become in recent years part of the research agenda of comparative political scientists, but research on these questions in relation to the countries of CEE has been almost absent. Thus, the book highlights the role of political parties in new political-economic systems. Scholarly work focusing on these new democracies has not provided political parties with agency when enacting economic reforms or reforms targeting education systems. Political parties have been largely overlooked. Valuable work has been done on the party systems in CEE (Grzymala-Busse 2007; Tavits 2009), but the link to the political economy literature has been weak.

3.5 Mapping the political economies of the European Union

The CEE political economies are mapped in three ways. First, we ask to which extent these economies fit the DME model. Second, these new market economies of CEE compare with a surprisingly similar set of countries in Latin America, thus putting the findings in a global context. Third, these findings are contextualized historically by speculating about their origin. Given the belief that "institutions need the continual political support of important political stakeholders in order to survive in the long term" (Hall and Thelen 2009: 12); institutions for skill formation are also analyzed historically in order to understand how they have been defined and re-defined (particularly in Chapters 3 and 4).

Recent work on the capitalist diversity of the CEE countries has quickly moved in the direction of contrasting the differences between them (Frye 2010; Bohle and Greskovits 2012). While this direction of research has been particularly relevant, the most striking common element seems to have been forgotten. Each country started its profound transformation from a (variety of) planned economy. This common evident characteristic should not be overlooked. The book depicts the consequences that derive from the common heritage of these economies. They all democratized and moved to a market economy simultaneously and relatively quickly, facing the triple challenges of democratization, marketization and welfare provision (Offe and Adler 1991).

At the same time, the findings are contextualized more globally. It includes discussion of its origins and its relationship both to the literature on dependency and to the HME model specifically. The HME model has been portrayed as characterizing Latin American countries (Schneider 2009). Ben Schneider (2009) developed the HME model at the same time as Nölke and Vliegenthart (2009) developed the DME model. In the HME formulation, domestic business conglomerates are the equivalent of MNCs in the DME model.

The origins of this variety of capitalism have remained unexplored. Research on the origins of capitalist systems – be these coordinated or liberal – includes substantial book-length studies (especially the works of Thelen [2004] and Streeck [2009]), such as this book cannot aim to achieve. However, this research touches upon the possible combination of factors that has led to the emergence of the DME model in CEE. It also aims to allow for an understanding of institutional change and the direction of this change (particularly in Chapters 3 and 4). We tackle why some governments had no incentives to steer these economies on a developmental path like that of the East Asian subcontinent. Governments strategies are linked to the preferences of their constituencies.

Lastly, the role of the Europeanization process in explaining these developments cannot be discounted. The Bologna reforms have had a major impact on HE dynamics across Europe (Dobbins 2011). This process should have influenced the countries equally – but we still notice differences between them, both within the ten country-sample and beyond. Governments implementing reforms did so while preserving their country specificity. At the same time, HE reforms in the region have taken place before the Bologna process started in 2002. Therefore, the increase in enrolment cannot be entirely linked to the Europeanization process. Bruszt and McDermott (2012) convincingly argue that the role of the European Union has been critical for certain sectors and industries, particularly in the dairy industry in Romania or Poland. The normative power of Europe, substantially supported by structural funds, has influenced HE governance. This is considered in each chapter of the book.

The European Union is another essential actor in upgrading processes in CEE. The European Union has provided a plausible institutional model, and this has been critical for the success of some Eastern European countries, such as Hungary, the Czech Republic and Poland. Dobbins (2011) focuses on the positive effects of Europeanization in HE. The processes through which international institutions influence domestic developments are complex (Bailer 2004). This can work by attaching conditions to funding or by imposing membership conditions. The World Bank or the International Monetary Fund can play a similar role (Pop-Eleches 2008). Nevertheless, it is still not clear why the European Union has had a strong influence on some countries but less on others. Domestic factors have made European policies more salient and effective in some countries than others. Indeed, Vachudova (2008: 861) acknowledges that political parties only respond to European Union requirements as long as this does not affect the domestic sources of their power.

4 Research methodology

Methodologically, this research combines several approaches. It follows career incentives, i.e. incentives for individuals to invest in education or to make decisions regarding their employment destination (i.e. abroad/domestically; private/public). Analyzing the world from the perspective of the individual offers a new perspective on this variety of capitalism and provides conceptual clarity.

The four steps of the mixed-methods strategy of the book are easily identifiable on the methodological map proposed by Lieberman (2005) for what he labels a nested analysis.

Concept formation is achieved in the within-case analysis of Romania. The research proceeds with a partial formalization of the model as part of the theory-building process and with testing some of the hypotheses derived from the case study within a quantitative framework and in a comparative case studies design. The research reveals both the *processes of interaction* of the relevant institutions and their *outcomes.*

4.1 Case study of Romania

The Romanian political economy provides a good context for analyzing the complexity of a DME because we would expect to see the DME model particularly clearly in this crucial case. We rely on the *inductive typical-case selection strategy* (Gerring 2007: 91). The case study serves two purposes: to formulate hypotheses and to provide internal validity. Internal validity is achieved through the ability to account for all the different factors that may affect the outcome of interest. External validity, i.e. the generalizability of the findings to the population of ten countries, is assured in the cross-sectional analysis. First, the economy continues to be relatively unsuccessful, with the Romanian GDP per capita being the second lowest in the European Union (after Bulgaria), but higher than that of the neighbouring countries further east. Second, the share of MNCs has considerably increased until 2012 (while the share of domestic companies in GDP has fallen), with the largest MNCs accounting for important shares of GDP. The proportion of people employed in MNCs, out of total business employment, reached 25 per cent in 2011 (Eurostat's FATS, 2012), this share is the second highest in the European Union, after Luxembourg. Third, the main means of raising capital is through FDI, with the Romanian government continuing to promote this as an adequate source of investment, amongst others, also for the privatization of state-owned companies in the energy sector. Enrolments in HE institutions have increased most, while the GDP has lagged behind.

The fieldwork revealed that changes in one sector, such as the liberalization of the education sector, were also reflected in other areas, such as the privatization of state-owned enterprises. This points towards the *co-evolution of institutions.* This raises a series of questions about the causal mechanisms at play during the processes of co-evolution dealt with in the empirical chapters. Given that the book rests on observational data, analytical narratives are used as building blocks of causal inference. This approach is also encouraged by Goertz and Mahoney (2012: 106), who consider "the intensive process tracing of selected cases as a complement to large-N research in contexts where experiments are impossible".

4.2 Cross-national analyses

Aiming to overcome the methodological divide between the quantitative and the qualitative paradigms, the book combines analytical narratives with large-n cross-sectional analyses given the understanding that "a good social science theory should not merely predict a particular relationship between independent and dependent variables, but it should also explain how and why these factors are related to one another" (Lieberman 2005: 442).

The statistical models in the Chapter 2 analyze employment destinations relying on firm-level data from the European Bank for Reconstruction and Development (EBRD). Country-fixed effects are used for the ten countries under scrutiny and allow an exploration of the variation in skill level across countries and its effects on attracting MNCs to the respective domestic economies.

The book also relies on the comparative cases approach, analyzing the cases of Hungary and Poland and Poland and Romania. Relying on Mill's method of similarity and of difference, the book moves on to explicit comparisons, thus increasing analytical leverage (Hancké 2009), allowing for controlled comparisons (Slater and Ziblatt 2013). Chapters 3 and 4 ask questions regarding the ability of some of the ten CEE countries to upgrade, to move up the ladder of economic sophistication. Methodologically, both chapters use a most similar cases design.

5 Argument in brief

The DME model serves as a tool for explaining HE developments to simplify an over-complex set of interdependencies. A model is always wrong, but useful (Clarke and Primo 2012). The model's assumptions are tested empirically. Once this is achieved, the interdependencies described here can be followed more easily. A further test of the validity of the model is to present it in a stylized, formalized way. This is achieved in Chapter 2 of the book.

5.1 The emergence of a low-skills equilibrium

Chapter 1 enquires as to what explains the inability of the Romanian market economy to develop high value-added activities despite having registered such high enrolment rates. Chapter 2 asks this same question in relation to the ten CEE countries. In the following, a condensed form of the line of reasoning is presented.

In the immediate aftermath of the fall of communism in 1989, it was not unquestionable that CEE countries would immediately embrace the norms of democracy and the market economy. The orientation of political elites towards the West should be understood in the context of a general delegitimation of the Left, but, most importantly, as an estimation of the immediate material benefits that the governments in power would profit from. This can be conceptualized as an approximation of the summed gains from direct sources of revenues stemming from the European Union, the World Bank (WB), or other Western democracies in the form of aid or loans, from better private management of companies, and from remittances, i.e. sources of revenue as a result of migration. These material gains, more so than endogenous growth, have allowed some CEE countries to grow economically immediately after 1990.

The desire of subsequent governments to attract FDI came on the back of the lack of capital and the struggle of governments to generate growth internally. This initial step (i.e. becoming heavily reliant on FDI as the main source of finance) led to a persistent reliance on FDI as the primary means of raising investment. Moreover, this translated into increasing competition for FDI, especially amongst developing economies, given their lack of alternative sources of capital.

MNCs are deemed to have a strong position in these domestic economies and expect a preferential taxation regime and other benefits, e.g. discretional exit and movement of capital. FDI is the main source of capital for new businesses and for refinancing existing businesses, such as most of the privatized state-owned companies. Given the central position of MNCs in the economy (which has generated oligopolies in most industries), innovative business is rather scarce (as the World Economic Forum repeatedly pointed out in its Global Competitiveness Reports 2010–2013). Furthermore, even within MNCs, innovation is transmitted top-down within the hierarchies of the company and is mostly not achieved in the subsidiary in a DME. These subsidiaries are mostly used as assembly platforms.

The HE system is geared towards delivering medium- to low-quality education also because of low levels of spending on this. Thus, the economy adapted towards becoming a producer of low- to medium-skilled manufactured goods, entrenched in a low-skills equilibrium. This low-skills equilibrium also reflects the scarcity of high-skilled jobs in the domestic market and adapts to its downward pressure on the level of skills. In turn, highly skilled individuals are ought to seek alternative jobs in the European common market (to which they have quasi-free access). Thus, the EU creates the opportunity for highly skilled individuals to move abroad, thus further contributing to the weakening of the highly skilled labour supply.

At the same time, this reduces the risk of social unrest through the fact that people who wish to have the opportunity to migrate and this reduces the pressure for change coming from voters. Governments keep the system going through various mechanisms. On the one hand, they give students and highly skilled individuals the opportunity to leave and allow the formation of fairly skilled individuals through a relatively egalitarian university system. On the other hand, governments continue seeking FDI by offering preferential regimes and thus in turn further reinforcing the dependency of the economy. On top of this, in the absence of unrest and with a picture of policy continuation, political stability underpins a strong business environment, in turn attracting further foreign investment, yet without treating the underlying problem of the low-skills equilibrium and the little domestic investment and development.

In the DME characterized by a low-skills equilibrium the demand for high skills stemming from companies active domestically is rather low. Moreover, the employers most likely to offer jobs for highly skilled individuals are MNCs (this is explained in more detail in Chapter 2, focusing on employment destinations).

5.2 Upgrading to higher-skills equilibria

At the same time, this research also seeks to understand under what conditions some countries in the region have managed to upgrade economically while others have not. Within DMEs, MNCs choose the investment destinations for their new branches on the basis of the skills they find in the destination economy once controlling for other sources of variation. This implies that several other equilibria can be achieved, ranging from low-skilled to medium- and high-skilled. While these equilibria are generally stable, governments can have a decisive role in elevating them. Governments can coordinate efforts, help increase HE enrolment in specific fields and attract companies conducting more sophisticated activities. Different governments across the region have done so, particularly those governmental parties catering to the voters active in the advanced sector of the economy.

5.3 An alternative world

The book argues that the link between MNCs and HE institutions has been mediated decisively by political parties. This can explain complex political economic developments. However, the theoretical proposition advanced here is, at times, in stark contrast to existing explanations in the literature. Probably the most prominent of these views is the one arguing that there is no direct or indirect connection between MNCs, HE and political parties (Bohle and Greskovits 2012). According to this perspective, each of these actors is making independent decisions and their incentives are not influenced by the actions of the other actors. In other words, MNCs will enter a country independent of the level of education in that economy determined by other considerations, such as state subsidies, for instance. Moreover, individual voters, students or employees will not adapt their strategies according to the world they are experiencing. This seems a rather implausible theoretical proposition. The differences across countries seem to suggest that MNCs are able and willing to move to neighbouring countries to rely on the human and physical infrastructure, while marketing their products in the countries nearby. Therefore, the argument according to which MNCs will move to a country independent of the human capital existing there in order to "exploit" the local market, i.e. to market their goods there, seems incomplete.

This book assumes a certain degree of rationality of the political-economic actors analyzed. However, it is most likely that the actors singled out as relevant in this book will not always act rationally. Nevertheless, the empirical results seem to confirm the rational mechanism proposed. This suggests that, in the long run, rationality can be assumed to be dominant. Another important view, closely linked to the discussions on a lack of connection between institutions, is that coordination and complementarity between institutions are not perfect. We cannot expect actors to be adapting their strategies instantly and to always understand what their best strategies are. Nevertheless, on the long run, and due to repeated interactions, this tends to happen.

A third approach argues that historical legacies should figure prominently and determine outcomes. According to this view, the differences between the levels of sophistication in the countries of CEE can be explained to be largely due to the different starting points in the democratization and marketization era in 1989. This starting point includes their HE systems and the industrial infrastructure that has been inherited. This is unquestionably relevant but cannot fully explain variation within countries at different points in time. Moreover, historical legacies do not exist on their own but need the agency of political actors in order to become effective.

6 Roadmap of the book

The four empirical chapters build on one another. Chapter 1 explains the deterioration of HE in Romania in the context of its post-1989 political economic development. It captures the evolution of enrolment, quality and funding as key macro-level indicators of the HE system. These dynamics are explained with reference to the incentives, at the micro level, for (prospective) students to invest in education. Understanding the incentive structure at the micro level is vital for comprehending the evolution of HE in the country, but also, more generally, for grasping the nature of the Romanian economy as a DME entrenched in a low-skills equilibrium.

Chapter 2 extends the analysis to ten countries in an attempt to explain the role of MNCs in the CEE economies. It argues that the supply of skills, i.e. increasing enrolments, can be explained by the structure of demand for high skills in these CEE markets. Indeed, the most relevant private employers in the market, MNCs, play the crucial role on the demand side for high skills, while the governments play the decision-making role on the supply side, by liberalizing HE. The preferences of different institutional actors and their links to one another are analyzed by using survey data on firms collected by the EBRD. The chapter shows that MNCs are more likely than domestic companies to employ HE graduates.

Chapters 3 and 4 entail paired comparisons: Hungary and Poland and Poland and Romania. They explain under what conditions some countries have managed to upgrade economically while others have not. Some countries that have inherited a relatively similar political-economic system have managed to escape a low-skills equilibrium and have taken a different role in the global production chain through the role played by political parties. Chapter 3 first describes the differences between R&D intensity and aggregate value added by sector of national GDP in CEE countries. Second, it argues that countries that have managed to upgrade have had powerful governments simultaneously attracting MNCs and steering the development of HE institutions towards developing more sophisticated activities.

Conclusions

The book explains some puzzling developments in the countries of CEE: an impressive increase in HE enrolment not associated with an equally strong economic growth. It identifies divergences between countries, and it links these differences to the role played by political parties in conjunction with MNCs in the region. It uses a mixed-methods framework, providing analytical narratives and cross-country analyses of individual-level data. It combines explanations with descriptions, while being deeply embedded in well-established research traditions and at the same time contributing to their development. It redefines the political economic model of the DME (Nölke and Vliegenthart 2009) and it provides avenues for testing some of its implications empirically.

By analyzing the links between factors that are not usually studied together, it contributes to the body of knowledge on a relatively under-studied region. Little has been known before in political science about the evolution of HE and its links to the labour market and political parties in government. At the same time, skill formation is an important topic that had received puzzlingly little attention in new democracies. Most ambitiously, we hereby push the debate on skill formation towards new territories. The book shows why it is illuminating to think about actors as the driving forces of difficult-to-understand political-economic developments such as the higher education reforms in CEE. At the same time, it aims to develop theories that can reach across time and space. This research should inform work on democratic institutions and open economies in general. It shows how, even in the less fertile environments, political parties can play a crucial role in economic governance and in providing the adequate environment for firms to upgrade. This is a contribution to scholarship on comparative politics more broadly, because it shows how partisan politics shapes public policy. It can be considered an optimistic portrayal of partisanship.

The book does not aim to be exhaustive in explaining these political economies. Data paucity has been an important challenge for this research, and also for the analysis of high-skilled migration in particular. Data triangulation has been helpful in partially overcoming this difficulty by relying on interviews, surveys, as well as macro-economic indicators. Future work should complement these findings by also analyzing trends in advanced capitalist countries. While the answers provided here are not complete, they can improve our understanding of the political economic determinants of HE reform and the consequences of these reforms for the sophistication level of European economies.

Notes

1 We rely on UNESCO data on *Gross Enrolment Ratio*, which is defined as the total enrolment within a country in a specific level of education, regardless of age, expressed as a percentage of the population in the official age group corresponding to this level of education.
2 Romania's GDP in 2013 was the second lowest after Bulgaria's. The low starting point in the transition cannot explain this outcome; in 1989, Poland's GDP was lower than that of Romania.
3 Bulgaria, Czech Republic, Estonia, Hungary, Latvia, Lithuania, Poland, Romania, Slovakia, Slovenia.
4 This is the latest available data for all countries.
5 Data retrieved from United Nations Conference on Trade and Development (UNCTAD), March 2014.
6 I am thankful to Laszlo Bruszt for raising this point to me. This argument is advanced by Piketty (2014: 29) for justifying the choice of France as a case study of inequality. France faced a demographic transition ahead of other countries.

References

Alexe, I. (2011) "The fourth wave: Brain drain, Romania and the Western World" [al patrulea val. migratia creierelor romanesti pe ruta romania-occident]. Translated from Romanian. Soros Foundation Bucharest.

Ansell, B. (2010) *From the ballot to the blackboard: The redistributive political economy of education*. New York: Cambridge University Press.

Bailer, S. (2004) "Bargaining success in the European Union: The impact of exogenous and endogenous power resources", *European Union Politics*, 5(1): 99–123.

Bandelj, N. (2008) *From communists to foreign capitalists: The social foundations of foreign direct investment in postsocialist Europe*. Princeton, NJ: Princeton University Press.

Bayer, L. (2018) “Orbán rails against foreign interests in closing campaign rally”, *Politico*, April 4. Available at: www.politico.eu/article/orban-rails-against-foreign-interests-in-closing-campaign-rally/ (Accessed: 29 August 2018).

Besley, T. and Persson, T. (2009) “The origins of state capacity: Property rights, taxation, and politics”, *American Economic Review*, 99(4): 1218–1244.

Bluhm, K. (2001) “Exporting or abandoning the ‘German model’?: Labour policies of German manufacturing firms in central Europe”, *European Journal of Industrial Relations*, 7(2): 153–173.

Bohle, D. and Greskovits, B. (2006) “Capitalism without compromise: Strong business and weak labor in Eastern Europe's new transnational industries”, *Studies in Comparative International Development*, 41(1): 3–25.

Bohle, D. and Greskovits, B. (2007) “Neoliberalism, embedded neoliberalism and neocorporatism: Towards transnational capitalism in Central-Eastern Europe”, *West European Politics*, 30(3): 443–466.

Bohle, D. and Greskovits, B. (2009) “Varieties of capitalism and capitalism”, *European Journal of Sociology*, 50(3): 355–386.

Bohle, D. and Greskovits, B. (2012) *Capitalist diversity on Europe's periphery.* Ithaca, NY: Cornell University Press.

Bruszt, L. and McDermott, G.A. (2012) “Integrating rule takers: Transnational integration regimes shaping institutional change in emerging market democracies”, *Review of International Political Economy*, 19(5): 742–778.

Buchen, C. (2007). “Estonia and Slovenia as antipodes” in Lane, D. and Myant, M. (eds.), *Varieties of capitalism in postcommunist countries*: 65–89. Basingstoke: Palgrave Macmillan.

Busemeyer, M.R. and Trampusch, C. (2011) “Comparative political science and the study of education”, *British Journal of Political Science*, 41(2): 413–443.

Busemeyer, M. and Trampusch, C. (2012) *The political economy of collective skill formation.* Oxford: Oxford University Press.

Campos, N.F. and Coricelli, F. (2002) “Growth in transition: what we know, what we don't, and what we should”, *Journal of Economic Literature*, 40(3): 793–836.

Cardoso, F.H. and Faletto, E. (1979) *Dependency and development in Latin America* [Dependencia y Desarrollo en America Latina, Engl.] Translated by Marjory Mattingly Urquidi. Berkeley: University of California Press.

Cernat, L. (2006) *Europeanization, varieties of capitalism and economic performance in Central and Eastern Europe.* New York: Palgrave Macmillan.

Clarke, K.A. and Primo, D.M. (2012) *A model discipline: Political science and the logic of representations.* Oxford: Oxford University Press.

Collier, D., LaPorte, J., and Seawright, J. (2012) “Putting typologies to work. concept formation, measurement, and analytic rigor”, *Political Research Quarterly*, 65(1): 217–232.

Crouch, C., Streeck, W., Boyer, R., Amable, B., Hall, P.A., and Jackson, G. (2005) “Dialogue on institutional complementarity and political economy”, *Socio-Economic Review*, 3(2): 359–382.

Dobbins, M. (2011) *Higher education policies in Central and Eastern Europe: Convergence towards a common model?* Hampshire: Palgrave Macmillan.

Docquier, F. (2006) *Brain drain and inequality across nations.* IZA DP No. 2440. Bonn: IZA.

Drahokoupil, J. (2008) *Globalization and the state in Central and Eastern Europe: The politics of foreign direct investment.* London and New York: Routledge.

Drahokoupil, J. (2009) "After transition: Varieties of political-economic development in Eastern Europe and the former Soviet Union", *Comparative European Politics*, 7 (2): 279–298.

Eurostat (2014) *Foreign affiliated statistics*. Brussels: European Commission.

Evans, P.B. (1979) *Dependent development: The alliance of multinational, state, and local capital in Brazil*. Princeton, NJ: Princeton University Press.

Feldmann, M. (2006) "Emerging varieties of capitalism in transition countries industrial relations and wage bargaining in Estonia and Slovenia", *Comparative Political Studies*, 39(7): 829–854.

Frye, T. (2002) "The perils of polarization: Economic performance in the post-communist world", *World Politics*, 54(3): 308–337.

Frye, T. (2010) *Building states and markets after communism: The perils of polarized democracy*. New York: Cambridge University Press.

Gerring, J. (2007) *Case study research: Principles and practices*. New York: Cambridge University Press.

Glaeser, E. (2011) *Triumph of the city: How our greatest invention makes US richer, smarter, greener, healthier and happier*. Basingstoke: Pan Macmillan.

Goertz, G. and Mahoney, J. (2012) *A tale of two cultures: Qualitative and quantitative research in the social sciences*. Princeton, NJ: Princeton University Press.

Grzymala-Busse, A. (2007) *Rebuilding Leviathan: Party competition and state exploitation in post-communist democracies*. Cambridge: Cambridge University Press.

Hall, P.A. and Soskice, D. (2001) *Varieties of capitalism: The institutional foundations of comparative advantage*. Oxford: Oxford University Press.

Hall, P.A. and Thelen, K. (2009) "Institutional change in varieties of capitalism", *Socio-Economic Review*, 7(1): 7–34.

Hancké, B. (2009) *Debating varieties of capitalism: A reader*. Oxford: Oxford University Press.

Hancké, B. (2011) "Endogenous coordination: Multinational companies and the production of collective goods in Central and Eastern Europe". LEQS Paper. London: London School of Economics and Political Science.

Hancké, B., Rhodes, M., and Thatcher, M. (2008) *Beyond varieties of capitalism: conflict, contradictions, and complementarities in the European economy*. Oxford: Oxford University Press.

Hanushek, E. A. and Woessmann, L. (2011) "How much do educational outcomes matter in OECD countries?" *Economic Policy*, 26(67): 427–491.

Hughes, J., Sasse, G., and Gordon, C. (2004) "Conditionality and compliance in the EU's Eastward Enlargement: Regional policy and the reform of sub-national government", *Journal of Common Market Studies*, 42(3): 523–551.

Iversen, T. and Soskice, D. (2001) "An asset theory of social policy preferences", *American Political Science Review*, 95(4): 875–893.

Iversen, T. and Soskice, D. (2009) "Distribution and redistribution: The shadow of the nineteenth century", *World Politics*, 61(3): 438–486.

Lieberman, E.S. (2005) "Nested analysis as a mixed-method strategy for comparative research", *American Political Science Review*, 99(3): 435–452.

Lindahl, M. and Krueger, A.B. (2001) "Education for growth: Why and for whom?" *Journal of Economic Literature*, 39(4): 1101–1136.

Mykhnenko, V. (2007) "Strengths and weaknesses of 'weak' coordination: Economic institutions, revealed comparative advantages, and socio-economic performance of mixed market economies in Poland and Ukraine," in Hancké, B., Rhodes, M. and

Thatcher, M. (eds.), *Beyond varieties of capitalism: Conflict, contradictions, and complementarities in the European economy*: 351–378. Oxford University Press.

Nölke, A. and Vliegenthart, A. (2009) "Enlarging the varieties of capitalism: The emergence of dependent market economies in East Central Europe", *World Politics*, 61(4): 670–702.

Offe, C. and Adler, P. (1991) "Capitalism by democratic design? Democratic theory facing the triple transition in East Central Europe", *Social Research*, 58(4): 865–892.

Pierson, P. (2004) *Politics in time: History, institutions, and social analysis.* Princeton, NJ: Princeton University Press.

Piketty, T. (2014) *Capital in the twenty-first century.* Cambridge, MA: Harvard University Press.

Polanyi, K. (1944) *1957: The great transformation*. Boston, MA: Beacon Press.

Pop-Eleches, G. (2008) "A party for all seasons: Electoral adaptation of Romanian Communist successor parties", *Communist and Post-Communist Studies*, 41(4): 465–479.

Pop-Eleches, G. (2009) "Public goods or political pandering: Evidence from IMF programs in Latin America and Eastern Europe", *International Studies Quarterly*, 53(3): 787–816.

Powell, J. and Trampusch, C. (2012) "Europeanization and the varying responses in collective skill systems", in Busemeyer, M.R. and Trampusch, C. (eds.), *The political economy of collective skill formation*: 284–313. Oxford University Press.

Rhodes, M. and van Apeldoorn, B. (1998) "Capital unbound? The transformation of European corporate governance", *Journal of European Public Policy*, 5(3): 406–427.

Sanchez-Ancochea, D. (2009) "State, firms and the process of industrial upgrading: Latin America's variety of capitalism and the Costa Rican experience", *Economy and Society*, 38(1): 62–86.

Sasse, G. and Thielemann, E. (2005) "A research agenda for the study of migrants and minorities in Europe", *JCMS: Journal of Common Market Studies*, 43(4): 655–671.

Schimmelfennig, F. and Scholtz, H. (2008) "EU democracy promotion in the European neighbourhood political conditionality, economic development and transnational exchange", *European Union Politics*, 9(2): 187–215.

Schimmelfennig, F. and Sedelmeier, U. (2005) *The Europeanization of Central and Eastern Europe.* Ithaca, NY: Cornell University Press.

Schmidt, V.A. (2009) "Putting the political back into political economy by bringing the state back in yet again", *World Politics*, 61(3): 516–546.

Schneider, B.R. (2009) "Hierarchical market economies and varieties of capitalism in Latin America", *Journal of Latin American Studies*, 41(3): 553–575.

Slater, D. and Ziblatt, D. (2013) "The enduring indispensability of the controlled comparison", *Comparative Political Studies*, 46(10): 1301–1327.

Streeck, W. (2009) *Re-forming capitalism: Institutional change in the German political economy.* Oxford: Oxford University Press.

Tarlea, S. (2017) "Higher education governance in Central and Eastern Europe: A perspective on Hungary and Poland", *European Educational Research Journal*, 16 (5): 670–683.

Tarlea, S. (2018) "Low-and high-skills equilibria in Central and Eastern Europe: What role for the government?" *East European Politics and Societies*: 0888325418777059.

Tarlea, S. and Freyberg-Inan, A. (2018) "The education skills trap in a dependent market economy. Romania's case in the 2000s", *Communist and Post-Communist Studies*, 51(1): 49–61.

Tavits, M. (2009) *Presidents with prime ministers: Do direct elections matter?* New York: Cambridge University Press.
Thelen, K. (2004) *How institutions evolve: The political economy of skills in Germany, Britain, the United States and Japan*. Cambridge: Cambridge University Press.
UNESCO (2014) *UNESCO Data on Education*. Paris: UNESCO Institute for Statistics.
Vachudova, M.A. (2008) "Tempered by the EU? Political parties and party systems before and after accession", *Journal of European Public Policy*, 15(6): 861–879.
Wallerstein, I. (1974) *The modern world-system: Capitalist agriculture and the origins of the European world-economy in the sixteenth century.* Berkeley: University of California Press.
World Economic Forum (2013) *Global Competitiveness Report 2013*. Available at: www3.weforum.org/docs/WEF_GlobalCompetitivenessReport_2013-14.pdf (Accessed: 29 August 2018).

1 Romania's dependent market economy

The role of higher education in setting up a low-skills equilibrium trap[1]

Introduction

We discuss the political economic development of Romania since 1989, with a focus on the evolution of higher education (HE). First, we place this evolution in the context of demand for HE by prospective students and employers, focusing on the low demand for skills in the multinational companies (MNC)-dominated Romanian economy. Second, we provide empirical insight on indicators of quality, enrolment, and funding as key features of the HE system. We argue that Romania has evolved into a dependent market economy (DME) entrenched in a low-skills equilibrium, and that the weakness of the HE system is a key element in this process.

Even if skills acquired in communist HE were overly specialized and not easily transferable (Boeri 2000), the system was creating "too many rocket scientists, too few marketing experts" (Campos and Dabusinskas 2002), and the social sciences, broadly defined, were altogether stymied, one of the advantages Romania, like other post-communist countries, inherited from the communist era was a relatively well-performing HE sector. The level of instruction in East and Central European universities was considered comparable to that in Western Europe (Graham 1987), at least in the hard sciences and mathematics (Tomusk 2000, 2004). Moreover, on human capital indicators such as enrolment or average years of schooling the former communist countries ranked close to the Organisation for Economic Co-operation and Development (OECD) (Barro and Lee 2001). This arguably meant that Romania, alongside other post-communist countries in Europe, commenced its transition to market economy with a relatively solid skills pool.

HE, through the complex skills it provides, is unquestionably vital for economic success in a knowledge-based society, on both individual and aggregate level (Goldin and Katz 2008; Krueger and Lindahl 2001; Hanushek and Wossmann 2010). The level of skills in an economy is *inter alia* positively correlated with the level of high value-added activities and innovation (McMullen, Mauch and Donnorummo 2000). While the aggregate level of skills depends on more than HE – it is, for example, also affected by vocational and on-the-job training – formal education remains a cornerstone.

In the context of transition, it was widely expected that the European post-communist economies would develop towards higher value-added activities. And a superficial glance at Romania might support such an impression. Macroeconomic indicators have continued to improve since 1990, entailing a considerable increase in GDP and living standards for a majority of the population, e.g. GDP/capita increased from US$1,600 in 1990 to US$9,500 in 2016 (IMF 2017). Successive post-communist governments have aimed to enhance competition on the education market, alongside other sectors (Dobbins and Knill 2009). Enrolment rates in Romanian HE institutions increased from 10 per cent in 1989 to 71 per cent in 2009, falling back to a still high 53 per cent in 2015 (UNESCO 2017). This seems broadly in line with Ansell's (2010) expectation that democratization and economic openness should lead to increased enrolment and funding for education.

Looked at more closely, three sets of factors combined during transition to lead us to expect a strong performance of the HE sector in Romania since 1989: (i) the country started marketization with a solid skills pool comparable to many advanced economies, and the number of competing institutions and enrolment only continued to increase thereafter; (ii) the period witnessed substantial and continued economic growth; (iii) the country started a democratization process, which implied increased responsiveness of governments to voters, who demand possibilities for upward mobility through education. However, the expectation of a strong performance in HE in post-communist Romania has in fact been met only partially. Instead, as we will show, HE quality has stagnated and even decreased, especially in technical subjects and in the hard sciences.

In this chapter, we analyze the role of HE in Romania post-89 in the context of the country's broader political-economic development. We argue that Romania has evolved into a DME trapped in a low-skills equilibrium, and that the lack of quality in HE is an element in this process.[2] Operationalizing and measuring the quality of HE is a most sensitive task. Evaluation procedures have not yet been developed at the European or a broader international level to assess the quality of HE, as opposed to the well-known OECD Programme for International Student Assessment (PISA) test for assessing education up to secondary level.[3] Drawing on the vast literature in education science (e.g. Harvey and Williams 2010), we recognize that assessments of HE quality ideally should be made in a differentiated manner, accounting for different stakeholders: students, employers, teaching staff, government and different funding agencies (Harvey and Green 1993: 10). HE quality has been conceptualized as fitness for purpose, as value for money or as transformative for the student (Harvey and Green 1993). However, given the scarcity of reliable and comparable data which could measure stakeholder-sensitive conceptualizations of HE quality in Romania, we must here proceed pragmatically: as will be further explained in Section 3, we provide information on all possible quality indicators on which systematic data exist while focusing most strongly on the relatively uncontroversial indicator of the ratio between absolute levels of funding and absolute levels of enrolment.

The lack of clear improvement of HE in post-communist transition is puzzling, but this puzzle has been largely overlooked in the literature, for at least three reasons. First, the legacy of a relatively high level of instruction took some time to wear off. It was not until the 2000s that stagnation or even decline became obvious to even domestic observers (Bucharest 2012; Ives et al. 2017). Second, government and education officials worked hard to project an image of success in westernizing education, both at home and abroad (Tomusk 2000). Third, observers (Deca 2015b) have often analyzed the capacity of the university system to "Europeanize" rather than its performance *per se* (an excellent example is Dobbins 2011).

Our analysis draws on a variety of sources, including access to Romanian-language policy documents, analyses and polls as well as a series of interviews with HE officials, politicians, academics and private-sector employees in human resources (HR) departments as well as focus groups with students and recent graduates (see references section for list of interviews). Respondents were selected from the range of stakeholders relevant for HE quality: academics in public and in private universities, students and young employees as well as employees in human resources departments, domestic and multinational employers, as well as representatives of think tanks and employers' associations.

The focus groups were conducted in the first stage of the data collection process to help generate and further develop hypotheses by means of general discussion. The results of the focus group discussions then subsequently informed the semi-structured interviews. Access to interviewees was facilitated through personal connections and the promise of confidentiality. This translated into an almost-100-per cent initial response rate. Response rates were lower once the snowball technique was used to gain access to other respondents but remained high at ca. 70 per cent. Only three interviews could be recorded, as this tended to be rejected, particularly in private companies. Records of all interviews are available upon request. Interview data were coded manually as encouraged by Saldana (2009) and analyzed thematically (using codes such as hiring principles, general vs. specific skills, funding for HE, study abroad etc.)

Information obtained from interviews was crosschecked with publicly available data as well as with secondary literature. Our narrative traces the links between the relevant actors and the process that has led to the outcomes described. We identify general trends from the interviews and find, e.g., that employers are very rarely interested in specific skills acquired at university and that university professors do not seem to have any incentives to restructure skills provision at university. Further methodological matters are clarified in each relevant section. Before proceeding to the analysis, however, an introduction to the DME concept is in order.

Nölke and Vliegenthart (2009), drawing attention to the impact of MNCs and international financial institutions on the institutional set-up of transition countries (see also Bandelj 2008; Drahokoupil 2009; Pop-Eleches 2009), have proposed a third political economy model next to the classic categories of coordinated (CME) vs. liberal market economy (LME) (Hall and Soskice 2001). This model, the DME, captures vital characteristics of much of post-communist Europe, and particularly of Romania. DMEs develop based on three linked factors: the presence of at least moderately skilled but cheap labour, the transfer of technological innovation within transnational enterprises and the provision of capital via foreign direct investment (FDI). We contribute to the development of this model by focusing on the crucial role of skills formation in a DME. Given the central role of FDI, in DMEs investment conditions and corporate governance are largely controlled by foreign, often multinational corporations. The local subsidiaries of MNCs in Eastern Europe are financed internally from within the company, and innovation within these MNCs tends to be transmitted top-down within the hierarchy of the company. Multinationals do not invest much domestically in R&D; they use DMEs as assembly platforms for innovations made at global headquarters and therefore rarely require highly skilled employees in the DME. At the same time, to attract MNCs DME governments will keep taxes low, which limits *inter alia* public spending on education. Ready to move on when profit margins fall, MNCs will not be in favour of a generous public education system funded by high taxes, nor will they themselves invest much in education or training.

We hold that Romania is a DME as typified by Nölke and Vliegenthart (2009), but we go further in characterizing Romania's variety of capitalism as specifically a low-skills type of DME. While DMEs can also operate at a medium-skills equilibrium with some competitive advantages (Nölke and Vliegenthart 2009) or evolve towards a coordinated or liberal type of political economy, neither of these trends is observable in contemporary Romania. Instead, with the end of economic transition the country emerges in a low-skills and low-productivity equilibrium, which is difficult to escape. The low-skills type of a DME is shaped by three prominent factors previously unlinked in the varieties of capitalism literature, which affect collective skill formation: the emigration of highly skilled individuals, low demand for highly skilled individuals in the domestic market, and a HE system whose features abet entrapment in DME status. In linking the evolution of HE to Romania's variety of capitalism, this chapter elaborates most fully on the last of these elements, while not leaving the others out of sight. We proceed by examining the incentive structure of (prospective) students and employers, focusing on employment and MNC business incentives, respectively. Our analysis reveals that growing enrolment in HE degree programs in Romania goes hand in hand with an increasing formalization of education, in which the actual skills transmitted do not count much for either employees or employers, and incentives to invest in improvement of HE quality are low on both sides. As a result, transformative effect, as an essential feature of HE quality, is low (Harvey and Green 1993).

The chapter is structured as follows: the next section offers an overview of incentives to invest in HE given the structure of demand for and supply of skills in the Romanian labour market. The argument is grounded in the broader analytical framework sketched previously, which characterizes Romania as a DME entrenched in a low-skills equilibrium. The third section shows how the evolution of HE after 1989 is explicable within this context, before the conclusion clarifies the broader relevance of our analysis.

1 Demand and supply of skills

1.1 Student demand

In this section, we present a simplified model of the incentives of (prospective) students to invest in obtaining HE, with the aim of explaining the observed high demand for HE at low levels of investment in quality (see Section 3). Understanding the motivations of students requires us to understand how they perceive their opportunities in the labour market. The decision tree in Figure 1.1 shows the most important decisions to be made by baccalaureate graduates. We have developed this decision tree based on the results of our focus group analyses and interviews, with the aim to capture students' perceptions of the incentives that determine their willingness to invest in obtaining quality HE. We also present data on objective indicators likely to affect these perceptions.

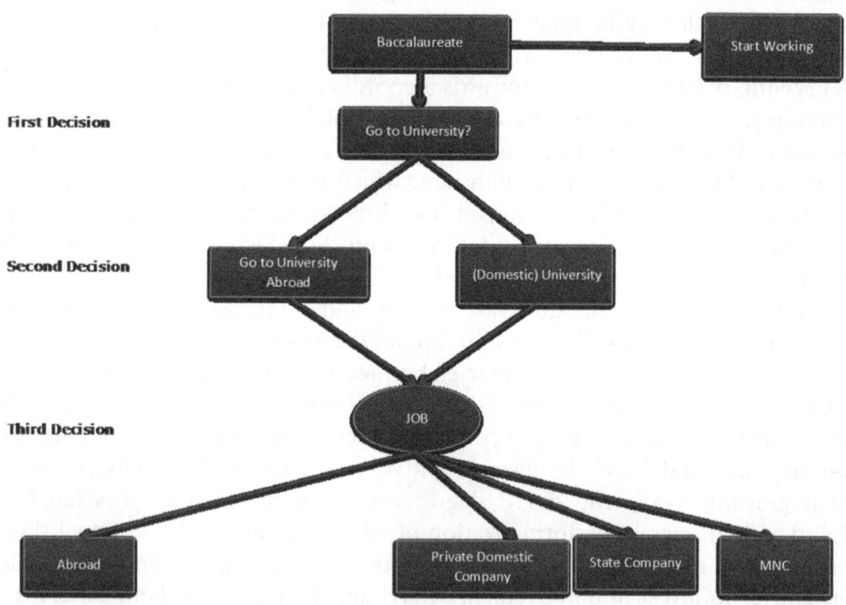

Figure 1.1 Decision tree for baccalaureate graduates

We here display decisions to be made by students regarding the first-degree program attended. The sequence is repeated when decisions need to be made about successive degree programs. This figure, which is informed by our focus group results, aims to bring order to complexity and represents a simplified version of the major options that students face. Real-life decisions are evidently not as straightforward as presented here.

Persons who have passed the baccalaureate exam are eligible to apply to universities. The *first decision* to be made is whether to go to university at all or to start working immediately. A large majority of Romanian students believe that receiving a HE degree will increase one's chances of earning good money – 80 per cent, e.g., according to a representative study conducted by the Romanian Agency for Quality Assurance in Higher Education (ARACIS 2010, Quality Barometer). Such findings are corroborated by the findings of our focus groups with current students. This supports the demand for HE degrees, as do various other factors supporting enrolment, discussed as follows.

The *second decision* to take is whether to go to university abroad or domestically. While in western European contexts the domestic-international divide between study locations may not be the most relevant, it is highly salient in Romania, given the universal perception that studying abroad guarantees better quality at considerably higher cost. This is supported by our focus group and interview results. The resulting HE brain drain (which also affects academic staff) contributes to the further weakening of the Romanian HE system. According to UNESCO data, the number of outbound mobile students (International Standard Classification of Education [ISCED] 5 and 6) has increased by 300 per cent between 1999 and 2016, by which time 33,000 Romanian students were studying abroad. The highest numbers of Romanian students were studying in Italy, France, Germany, the UK and the US. These figures are striking also in comparison across the region. Only two countries have comparable numbers of students studying abroad: in Poland, the number of students decreased from 30,000 in 2010 to 24,000 in 2016, and in Slovakia, 31,000 students were studying abroad in 2016 (UNESCO 2017).

The *third decision* is whether to work abroad or domestically after graduation, independent of where the HE degree has been obtained. A second wave of brain drain pulls highly skilled labour out of Romania. This is facilitated by improved access of highly qualified graduates to the European common market. Migration is attractive to many Romanian undergraduate students. Fifty per cent of the interviewees in the *Quality Barometer* (ARACIS 2010) declared that they intend to move to a different country, while 56 per cent intended to study abroad. Of course, students or graduates can always make a decision to return, which has the potential to improve the pool of available skills at home. However, as this chapter argues, this is made less likely by the limited demand for high skills in the domestic market.

Hence, an interesting consequence of European Union membership, which brings free access to the European HE market, is that this can have the unintended negative effect of lowering incentives for demanding quality education at home and, in this way, represent a threat to the development of HE in Romania. However, as our interviews revealed, this problem is generally not recognized by representatives of HE institutions in Romania, who instead perceive Romania's European Union membership as having a positive influence on HE in the country. Competition on the European HE market takes place outside the field of vision of the representatives of Romanian HE institutions. They focus instead on attracting as many students as possible from the already truncated pool of domestic students (Interview U5).

If students decide not to leave the country, their willingness to invest resources, including effort, in quality education declines as the opportunities they see for applying high-level skills in the labour market decline. At the same time, the easier it is to attend university (e.g. the lower admissions criteria, the lower tuition and the greater possibilities to work while studying), the more students will decide to go to university in order to obtain a formal degree. Essentially, they see that obtaining a degree is relatively easy, while not obtaining one is likely to diminish their chances, given the general run on HE degrees and the difficulty of obtaining well-paid work. The combination of easy access to universities and perceived lack of opportunities in the labour market increases the likelihood that young baccalaureate graduates will decide to attend a HE institution but will not be willing to invest significant resources either towards working for a quality education or towards creating effective political demand for quality HE. In short, baccalaureate graduates feel the need to obtain formal HE degrees to improve their employment opportunities, but do not expect that it will actually do so by improving their skills; they do not expect that HE will have a transformative effect. This supports a low willingness to invest in HE and thereby a continuing low quality of output of HE institutions.

Going back to the decision tree in Figure 1.1, we consider another potential factor that can help higher value-added activities emerge: entrepreneurship. This is a channel through which economic sophistication can increase and through which businesses can diversify existing portfolios. The extent to which entrepreneurship is present amongst the population of the country should be informative in this regard. A 2016 survey regarding Romanian entrepreneurship including opinions of 350 entrepreneurs, of which 45 per cent of business people with turnovers of over €10 million (Survey regarding Romanian entrepreneurship in 2016, [Ernst & Young – Raiffeisen Bank 2016]) shows that entrepreneurship is considered a viable path. Five pillars are considered in this survey: taxes and regulation, access to finances for start-ups, entrepreneurship education, coordinated support from the government and a culture appreciative of entrepreneurship. Seventy-three per cent of the surveyed entrepreneurs were over 40. Only a quarter of these entrepreneurs considered that Romania would offer a friendly business environment for entrepreneurs in five years' time; the assessment of the business environment was more positive over a ten-year period. Seventy per cent considered the instability of the legislative framework to be an obstacle for the development of their business. Fifty-one per cent of these entrepreneurs considered that the fiscal environment had improved, though. The survey also revealed that they were more optimistic in 2014, compared to 2016. Sixty-one per cent of interviewees suggested that their education in Romania did not prepare them to be successful entrepreneurs. Interestingly, interviewees also suggested that start-ups would be the best supported by governmental programs rather than other private initiatives, including funders willing to invest.

1.2 Employer demand

The motivations of students cannot be understood without taking into account the opportunities they perceive on the labour market. These, in turn, depend on Romania's more general political-economic development and the demand for skills stemming from employers. At the same time, employers are important stakeholders in the quality of HE. Their perceptions are considered in this section.

In the immediate aftermath of the fall of communism, Romanian governments and companies active domestically largely failed to realize domestic opportunities for growth. GDP declined dramatically while Romania had not yet opened up to FDI. Poor liquidity combined with the ideational dominance of the neoliberal model pushed subsequent governments to prioritize attracting FDI (Stark and Bruszt 1998). As Drahokoupil (2009) shows, by around the year 2000 state strategies in CEE generally converged towards competition for FDI. At the same time, foreign investors became more active in the region once countries had demonstrated consistent commitment to market economic and democratic transition over a decade. This led to foreign control of leading export industries and public utilities as well as to unprecedented levels of foreign dominance in the banking sector across the region after 2000 (Epstein 2014).

The importance of foreign companies in Central and Eastern Europe and in Romania in particular stems from two sources: they have become a main source of capital, so their share in capital formation is high – as suggested by FDI data, but, even more important, they have become key employers in these economies. According to Eurostat data (EBRD – World Bank 2017; EBRD – World Bank 2017), MNCs in Romania accounted for more than a quarter of business employment in 2015. Similarly, in 2015 around 23 per cent of the value added at factor cost in Romania was produced by MNCs (Eurostat 2017). These figures are not unusual for Central and Eastern Europe but higher than in any non-post-communist European country, except Luxembourg (Marginson and Meardi 2009, who use data from the European Industrial Relations Observatory).

In Romania, foreign-owned companies and in particular MNCs have become strong in terms of turnover and profit shares as well as employment in both goods and services, e.g. in public utilities, manufacturing (cement, metal, machine building, petroleum), as well as in financial brokering and trade (Chivu 2009). They dominate especially in the category of large companies (over 1,000 employees) and in services. In 2007, employment in private MNCs with more than 1,000 employees amounted to 51.4 per cent of total employment in private companies with more than 1,000 employees across the economy (41.3 per cent in manufacturing, 64.2 per cent in services) (Chivu 2009, based on National Statistics Institute [NSI] data). MNCs attract qualified labour by means of higher salaries and higher status than those offered by domestic companies. Also, the turnover per person employed has been significantly higher in MNCs compared to total business employment: in MNCs it ranged between €112,000 and €104,000 per year/employee between 2008 and 2010, whereas in total business employment the figures lay between €58,000 and €57,000 per year/employee.[4] The revenue-employee ratio has thus at times been twice as high in MNCs compared to total business employment (FATS statistics Eurostat 2017). This could lead one to expect that demand for the most sophisticated skills would stem from these MNCs. This also seems indicated in a survey conducted by the European Bank for Reconstruction and Development (EBRD) in all post-communist transition economies, which shows that the proportion of employees with HE degrees is substantially higher in MNCs compared to domestic companies (EBRD –World Bank 2015). However, in Romania we can see that this has not benefited the quality of the domestic HE system. We will now proceed to explain why.

Relevant scholarship focusing on the region has emphasized the dual role of MNCs for the development of its economies (Bohle and Greskovits 2012). According to the tenor of this literature, while they bring in much-needed capital, foreign investors tend to be short-term profit-oriented; they are unwilling to invest directly, or indirectly through higher taxation, into educating the labour force, while their strong position in the regional economies guarantees them preferential tax regimes and other benefits, such as discretionary exit of capital. Simultaneously, as we show in the following, in Romania the public education system is underfinanced, and education outcomes are correspondingly weak on the whole. The aggregate skill level of graduates of tertiary education institutions – certainly once we have subtracted those who are drawn abroad or into MNCs – is not high enough to enable significant domestic innovation. Over the past two decades, the lack of highly skilled labour, combined with the lack of domestic capital, has contributed to preventing home-grown economic development through domestic investment and business, turning Romania into a DME.

MNCs in Romania expect a moderately skilled workforce and are able to draw the better qualified away from domestic companies. However, within MNCs innovation tends to be transmitted top-down within the company hierarchy, rather than being achieved in the domestic subsidiary. According to the *Global Competitiveness Report* (GCR) produced by the World Economic Forum (2017a), which rests on nationally representative samples of private companies that are comparable across countries, Romania ranks 107th amongst 144 economies on the combined factors innovation and sophistication – last in the European Union. Local suppliers in Romania rank low in both quantity and quality. The national economy's competitive advantage (rank 104th out of 144) lies closer to low-cost products and natural resources. The country's capacity to attract or retain talent is ranked 132th out of 144 countries (World Economic Forum 2017b).

Dynamics more than 25 years into the transition in Romanian academia do not seem to suggest a change away from this DME status. Data from a 2016 employers' survey in Romania shows the difficulty of employers in finding suitable employees who have just graduated from university. Seventy per cent of the 450 interviewees find it difficult to hire graduates fresh out of university. Looking at this at a more disaggregate level shows that it is more difficult to find suitable candidates in economics, biomedical sciences and engineering than in mathematics or informatics. This seems to emphasize that the existing demand for sophisticated skills, no matter how weak, is difficult to meet by the existing skill pool. Hence, the expectation that the existing skills would allow for an upgrading seems not to be met (EBRD – World Bank 2017).

According to data from the Directorate General Research Annual Report of 2011, Romania ranked 26th in the EU 27 on share of research-and-development-related activities in GDP, 25th on the share of high-tech exports in total exports, and 27th on European patent applications. Scientists and engineers constituted a mere 4.3 per cent of the labour force (18th place in the European Union). Expenditure on research and development as a percentage of GDP has been lower than 0.5 per cent between 2008 and 2016 (compared to, e.g., around 1 per cent in Poland and 1.2 per cent in Hungary (Eurostat 2017; Tarlea 2017). Data on the percentage of GDP spent on R&D by private companies also supports the thesis of a low-skills equilibrium (Eurostat, Structural Business Statistics). The low skill level in the Romanian economy is also reflected in its employment structure (see Figure 1.5 in Appendix). Next to its large agricultural sector (Romania has the highest agricultural production as part of GDP amongst the new European Union members; see Figure 1.2), most of which consists of small-scale agriculture, manufacture, construction, as well as wholesale and retail make up the bulk of employment. The data in Figure 1.2 is measured in thousand people. Only 1.6 per cent of the labour force are categorized by the NSI as being in professional, scientific or technical employment. Other categories in which HE graduates are routinely employed (public administration, health, education, IT and finance) add up to an additional 16.4 per cent. Moreover, the total number of employees has decreased between 2007 and 2016 from 9.3 million to 8.4 million people, and the sophistication level of economic activities is decreasing in Romania, unlike in the majority of the new European Union member states.

But even if the actual demand for high-level skills in the labour market is relatively low, enrolment in HE remains high while formal degrees are still

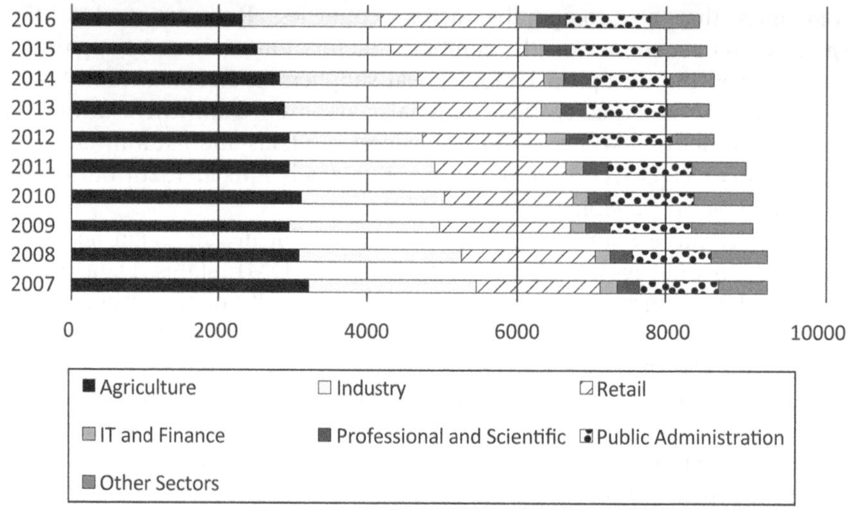

Figure 1.2 Romanian employment structure, per thousand people
Source: Eurostat 2017.

perceived as important by (prospective) employees and employers. In line with a Europe-wide trend, it is unlikely that enrolment rates will significantly drop, but we can already propose at this point that the demand for HE in Romania is focused more on its formal than on its substantive value. Having sketched the peculiar demand structure for HE degrees, we now turn to considering the supply of HE in light of these parameters.

1.3 Governmental responses to the skills demand structure

After 1989, Romania witnessed an exceptional increase in HE enrolment (see Figure 1.3).

There are several reasons for the increasing enrolment in HE during the period. One is the growth of the student-age cohort in the 2000s. The student age cohort continued to grow until 2009, when the first cohort born after the cancellation of Romania's anti-abortion legislation came of age. In absolute terms, in 1990 the number of persons enrolled in university lay at 200,000; this had reached 900,000 in 2008 and decreased to 800,000 in 2010. By now HE enrolment has stabilized at a high level which seems resistant even to a declining overall population and student age cohort.

A second reason for increasing demand, which was repeatedly mentioned in our interviews with Romanian academics, is that the public administration increasingly required a tertiary education degree for positions for which secondary education degrees would have sufficed in the past. This process has been driven by European Union accession conditionality and the necessity to align the state bureaucracy with the *acquis communautaire*. It became common practice for state employees to seek degrees, mostly in business and

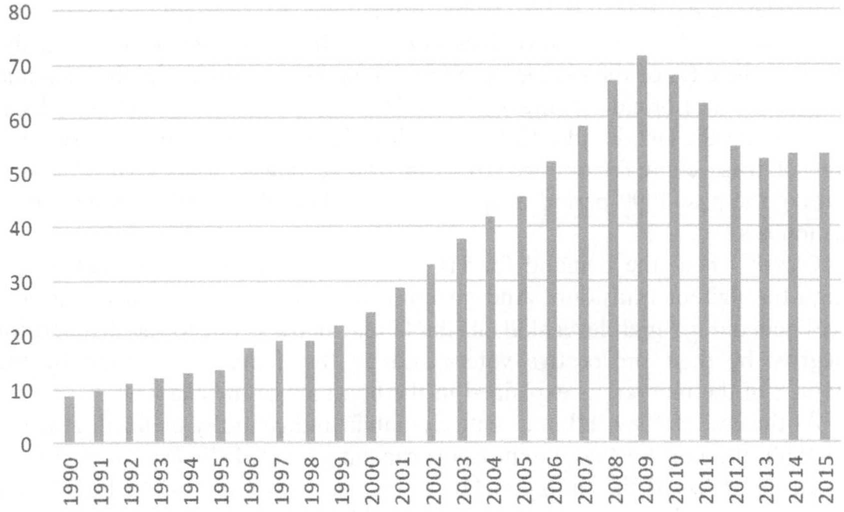

Figure 1.3 Gross enrolment rates in higher education, Romania
Source: UNESCO 2017.[5]

law, to be able to keep their positions. This type of demand is, however, not created by an increasing need for skills (or a change in required skill structures), but rather by an increasing need for formal degrees. It therefore helps account for the continuing increase in demand for HE degrees independent of the quality of the education provided.

Third, the expansion and diversification of employment opportunities on the private market also help explain the increasing demand for HE, as many positions in international but also domestic private firms require, or are more easily accessed with, a HE degree. Fourth, and often in combination with the previously outlined reasons, the high unemployment rates that characterized much of the transition period motivated some individuals to remain in or go back to school rather than face the threat of unemployment. Fifth, the opportunity cost of attending universities has decreased during the period, as universities have spread to more locations, long-distance learning opportunities have multiplied and possibilities for combining work and studies have generally improved. Sixth, HE enrolment has profited from the significant drop in vocational training experienced in Romania during the same period. In comparison, "a strong and attractive vocational sector in some countries, such as Austria and Germany, helps explaining why fewer students are drawn to the tertiary education system" (Economic Policy Committee and Directorate-General for Economic and Financial Affairs 2010: 94).

A seventh factor to explain the increasing demand for HE might be lagged demand. Study places in HE had been kept artificially scarce during communism and were therefore overvalued at the beginning of transition. According to one university dean and member of European Parliament

(Interview U4), this has led many Romanians to overlook the fact that acquiring a HE degree today does not bear the same significance as it did back in the days of the planned economy. Last but not least, eighth, Romania finds itself in a broader context of worldwide massification of tertiary education during the last decades (Interview U6). There is no reason to suspect that any of these eight factors are irrelevant for keeping enrolment in HE high during the post-1990 period in spite of the decline of its quality, documented as follows.

Clearly, then, the demand for HE degrees by prospective graduates was high throughout transition. And governments responded, even if not to any real demand for high-level skills in the labour market, but to the demand for degrees by their prospective voters and by the demand generated by the MNCs in the market, as explained in the first part of the chapter.

At the end of 1989, HE was entirely public and centrally planned. Already in 1990, the first post-communist government provided the legislative framework that allowed the supply of HE to increase, *inter alia* by the foundation of private institutions, which spread rapidly across Central and Eastern Europe (CEE) more generally (Galbraith 2003). By 2009, Romania hosted 106 universities: 56 of them public, 50 private. In 2009, universities offered more student places than the total number of baccalaureate graduates in the country – a clear case of oversupply even given the quite consistent growth in bottom-up demand for HE.

The expansion of supply was driven by the recognition among politicians that legislative changes to facilitate the foundation of private universities would please both prospective students and their families and education

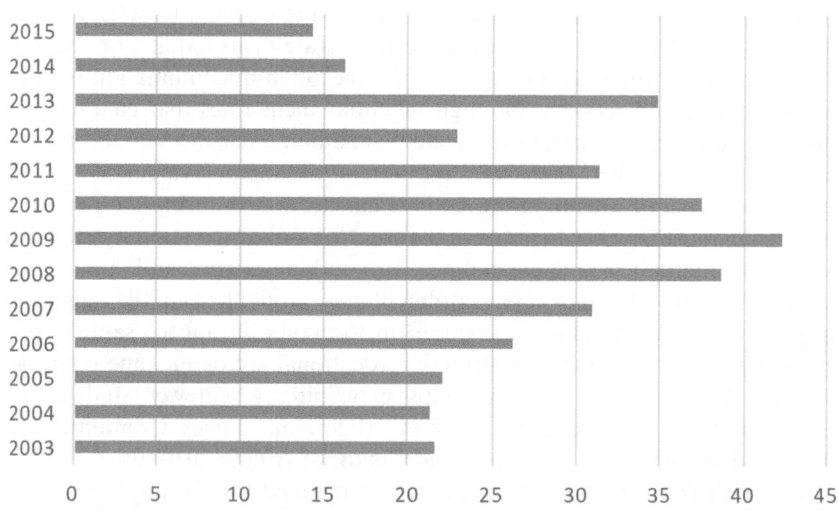

Figure 1.4 Enrolment in private higher education in Romania (percentage of total enrolment)
Source: UNESCO 2017.

entrepreneurs. According to an expert at the Bologna Secretariat in Bucharest, private universities have had a strong lobby in the Romanian legislature and government (Interview N5 April 2012). They have also contributed rather substantially to the state budget. According to data from the Romanian Ministry of Finance, for example, the private university Spiru Haret University in Bucharest made a profit of €42 million in 2008, €40 million in 2009 and €25 million in 2010 (Mihai 2011). The increasing supply of HE thus opened up a new field of profit generation while responding to the demand structure sketched previously.

After 2009, enrolment in private HE started to decline. This can be explained by (a) the decline in the student age cohort, which is also visible in slightly declining enrolment in public universities around the same time; (b) the increasing number of students studying abroad and (c) public universities becoming able to accommodate a larger share of the students, especially by providing "private" study places. The latter factor was another profit-generating part of the expansion of HE supply. Since 1993, public universities collect tuition fees according to the "numerus clausus" principle. Students ranked lower on the admissions criteria or those studying for a second degree pay fees. As a result, privatization of HE as a broader trend has also encompassed public universities. Private HE in Romania is provided by both private and public institutions, and public institutions typically contain both "public" (state-funded) and "private" (fees paying) students.

Private universities and private study places at public universities have benefitted students who would otherwise not have been admitted to HE. Academics could supplement their earnings by taking an extra job, and education entrepreneurs founded universities to make a profit. Also important was that private HE institutions presented themselves as an alternative to public HE at a time when the privatization of state-owned companies in most sectors of the economy was publicly endorsed and officially pursued by the government. The broader context of privatization thus helps explain the uncontested emergence of private HE institutions and "private" study places at public institutions.

Given the increasing demand, potential HE providers with entrepreneurial skills (and the required access to important networks) have seen opportunities in starting up private institutions as an alternative to state-financed universities. They soon outperformed public institutions in terms of enrolment levels.[6] Their marketing strategy across the board was to compete with existing public HE institutions on lower prices (than fees-paying positions in public universities), laxer entrance criteria and the promise of passing exams more easily, and not on exclusiveness and higher quality programs. While they increasingly represented competition for publicly funded universities, this competition failed to boost quality, as public universities by and large chose to compete with private institutions on their own terms: public universities also moved in the direction of attracting more students and have thus become less exclusive and, increasingly, only formally quality-oriented. The alternative strategy available to public universities, one of stressing exclusivity and quality, was not chosen, as will be further discussed in the next section.

2 The political economy of HE quality

So far, we have emphasized the increasing proliferation of HE recipients in the Romanian market, analyzing the determinants of both the demand and the supply side for skills. Understanding these determinants underscores that counting the number of HE degrees is a poor assessment of the state of HE in a political economy. A reasonable assessment should take into account the *quality* of HE processes and the (domestic and international) credibility of the degrees obtained. Marketization, democratization and an institutional preoccupation with HE quality could conceivably have led to an increase in HE quality. However, the Romanian case does not bear out the expectation of improving quality of HE through competition and employer demand. There has been little specialization, and the quality of HE, especially but not only in private institutions, is poor. As one of our interviewees (U5), an academic from a public university, lamented: "Engineering is decaying in Romania, while the world is becoming more technologically advanced."

As Jones and Ratcliff (1999) point out, there is no international consensus on what constitutes quality in HE, because the proper goals and means of such education are highly context- and stakeholder-dependent. As a result, comparing the quality of HE in Romania over time, not to mention during and after communism, is a difficult endeavour. Also, any assessment of the quality provided by an education system must take into account the domestic as well as international institutional constraints, such as quality assurance mechanisms, faced by such a system, such as the ARACIS in Romania's case. Our biggest difficulty for this particular chapter, however, is the absence of systematic over-time data. These difficulties call for a flexible approach to capturing the quality of HE which uses multiple indicators to triangulate individual measurements and to allow for multiple comparisons, relying on different (combinations of) indicators, with a variety of other places and times.

Hence, drawing on Tomusk (2000) and on Harvey and Green (1993), we here assess in brief four different factors to capture the quality of HE in Romania as it has evolved since 1989: (1) student-teacher ratio, (2) academic scholarship output, (3) students' perceptions regarding the development of their skills in the HE system and (4) institutional efforts to improve HE quality. Factor (1) is an input factor for HE, whereas (2) and (3) are output factors (research and teaching). Factor (4) depends strongly on the financing of HE, which is possibly the most important input factor.

First, from the points of view of both students and teachers, within certain limits, a lower student-teacher ratio improves the educational experience that can be provided. The student-teacher ratio in Romanian HE increased from 13.8 students/teacher in 1990 to 19 in 2001, 21.5 in 2005, a high of 28 in 2009 and 25 in 2010. By 2015, it had decreased to 20 due to the lower enrolment rates (UNESCO 2017).

The second factor we consider is output of academic scholarship in the form of publications or patents and citations by other scholars. Such measurements are questionable in many ways, as the statistics in use measure directly the quantity and publicity value of certain categories of publications, rather than their quality or a scholar's more general contribution to his or her field (see e.g. van Vught and Ziegele 2012 for a critique). Yet in the absence of other systematic data we will here report the available data on research output.

To assess research output in Romania today it is important to recognize that universities in communist CEE were generally focused relatively more on teaching and relatively less on research. This has led some scholars to conclude that Romania still employs a "teaching model" today, similarly to Bulgaria, Lithuania or Latvia (St. Aubyn et al. 2009). But this is misleading, because after 1990, Romanian academia slowly started at least a formal reorientation towards an increasing status for research. The number of citable documents (articles, reviews and conference papers) produced by scholars affiliated with Romanian HE institutions has steadily increased, according to the SCImago database, from around 1,838 documents in 1996 to 10,897 documents in 2010. Romania's h index was 201 in 2016. This means that at least 201 articles published in Romania between 1996 and 2016 have received at least 201 citations. On this measure, Romania ranks 42nd in the world out of 238 countries, lower than, e.g., the less populous Czech Republic or Hungary. We can derive from the data that Romanian visible research output has increased significantly, in line with a general trend observed for all 238 countries in the ranking, but it has increased less than in other countries in the region. The relative scarcity of internationally visible research output is also documented by Deca (2015a). Furthermore, frequent cases of academic dishonesty have damaged the reputation of Romanian research output. Ives et al. (2017) provide a thorough discussion of this problem, also in light of the 2015 plagiarism allegations against prime minister Victor Ponta.

Third, as regards students' views on their skills development, in a survey conducted in 2004 by Gallup for the British Council a majority of young people (ages 15–35) expressed dissatisfaction with textbooks and curricula (not modern nor adapted to market needs), assessment methods (do not accurately evaluate knowledge) and didactic methods (do not actively involve students). Current university students, as compared to high school pupils or those who had completed their formal education, were especially critical on all counts (British Council 2004). The Quality Barometer on HE in Romania shows for the years 2009, 2010 and 2011 that the average confidence of students in the quality of HE in Romania is very low (4 out of 10 on a scale from 0 – no confidence to 10 – high confidence), much lower still than that of employers, which in turn is lower than the confidence of professors. Students from 40 Romanian universities were polled in 2009, 2010 and 2011.

The sample was representative for students nationwide (ARACIS 2010); unfortunately, this is the most recent available data.

The reasons for the poor quality of HE in Romania are numerous and complex. The most frequently made argument is that the poor financing of HE can explain its weak performance (Miroiu and Aligica 2008). But why is then not more money being spent? Based on the demand structure explained previously, we argue that governments do not have any incentives to improve the financing of HE given the structure of the economy and the motivations of students to pursue a degree. The Romanian HE sector has consequently been chronically underfinanced, as spending on education overall and on HE in particular has remained low, even while enrolment continued to skyrocket. Between 2010 and 2012 about 4 per cent of GDP was spent on education in general, compared to an OECD average of 6.1 per cent and a European Union average of 5.1 per cent (in 2008, the last year for which consolidated information exists). While the Romanian Education Law (no. 1/2011, Article 8) stipulates that a minimum of 6 per cent of GDP should be spent on the education system; this stipulation has so far not been implemented, and there are no signs that it will be taken more seriously in the near future. As regards spending on HE more specifically, based on UNESCO data, the total expenditure on HE institutions in Romania – both public *and private* – as percentage of GDP was 0.88 per cent in 2002, 1.24 per cent in 2005 (of which 0.42 per cent from private sources) and 1.61 per cent in 2007. In comparison, in 2005 Poland was spending 1.6 per cent of GDP on HE, Estonia 1.2 per cent and Lithuania 1.4 per cent.[7] Expenditure per student (measured as per cent of GDP/capita)[8] has decreased from 32.5 per cent in 2001 to 26.2 per cent in 2002, 22.1 per cent in 2004, 26.1 per cent in 2007 and 23.4 per cent in 2014, according to the World Bank (2017).

Besides being low, the way in which public funds for HE have been distributed after 1989 has not created incentives to invest in improving the quality of education or research. Aiming to address the problems stemming from insufficient funding, in 1993 the government allowed public universities to collect tuition fees according to the "numerus clausus" principle (creating "private" study places). At the same time, in line with a Europe-wide trend, public funds began being distributed mostly according to enrolment levels.[9] Most private funds are directly enrolment-dependent, as they are collected through tuition fees from students willing to pay for their education. The main goal of HE institutions of all types has consequently become to increase enrolment. This was emphasized in our interviews as well: "Everything was about numbers, this was all that mattered" (Interview 5). Since 2002, public funds have been distributed based on a formula with both quantitative and qualitative elements. A qualitative component, referring mostly to national and international research output as well as to the capacity to attract research funding, is also part of the formula. If a faculty scores well on the quality criteria, it receives part of the funding based on this score. However, the results in terms of quality improvements have been modest, as only a very small part of the funding is being distributed this way.

Competition over students, driven by these financing mechanisms as well as oversupply of study places, instead of supporting a race to the top between institutions, has instead served to keep the price of education low. While prices in Romania have increased across the board, HE remained relatively cheap (Miroiu and Aligica 2008). From 1990 to 2010 tuition fees ranged between the equivalent of €300 and €500 per year, in private universities and paid for study places in public universities.

Still, it is puzzling that fees are low for *all* universities, that there is no differentiation and no entrepreneurs have tried to create elite institutions. Miroiu and Aligica (2008) suggest that this is due to the manner in which HE is subsidized by the state, which does not allow it to become more expensive and therefore more valuable. But this neoliberal argument cannot explain the developments in the private components of the HE sector. We argue instead that the state of HE in the country overall can be better explained by the nature of the *demand* for HE in a low-skills DME context, to which we now return.

Conclusions

In Romania, HE is geared towards delivering low to medium quality education, while the economy is geared towards producing manufactured goods and services requiring low to medium-skills – in short, Romania is entrenched in a low-skills equilibrium (Finegold and Soskice [1988] use this concept in relation to the UK). This is an equilibrium state, because it both reflects the scarcity of high-skilled jobs in the domestic market (given the strong role of MNCs) and serves to keep the aggregate level of skills in the domestic economy low. Highly skilled individuals can compete with non-Romanians for high-level positions in international companies or organizations. They may also aim for domestic employment, such as in the medical profession or as university professors. However, salaries in the professions are very low, especially in the public sector, which drives many top-qualified candidates away. Alternatively, they seek employment abroad, most often on the European common market, to which they now have open access (Alexe 2011). The fact that European Union membership creates opportunities for the few highly skilled to develop further abroad, through education and work, further lowers the supply of highly skilled labour at home.

Improved "exit" options from the Romanian HE and labour markets also reduce the pressure for change coming from voters. Successive governments have maintained the same set of parameters governing HE and its role in the political economy. They have worked to improve the opportunities for students and highly skilled individuals to leave the country while maintaining the formation of moderately skilled individuals through a relatively egalitarian and accessible but chronically underfunded and badly regulated university system. They have simultaneously worked to attract FDI by offering a fairly stable business environment and preferential taxation and regulation, reinforcing Romania's economic dependency on capital and innovation from abroad. In the process, the twin problems of stunted domestic investment and development and low investment in HE on both the supply and the demand sides remain unaddressed. There is a real risk of recursiveness, as the nature of the HE system supports entrapment in DME status, and vice versa.

We began from the premise that the political-economic implications of the deterioration of HE in Romania since 1989 can be better understood by exploring the dynamics of demand and supply of HE and high-level skills in the Romanian economy. We have argued that a low-skills equilibrium has emerged in the country, in which a moderately educated population is producing low value-added goods and services. This is not only a symptom of Romania's status as a DME but also helps explain the failure to overcome the quality deficiencies of the post-communist Romanian HE system.

Our analysis has shed some light on why democratization and marketization have – contrary to Ansell's (2010) expectation – not had the effect of strengthening HE and might well fail to have this effect also elsewhere, if the general conditions identified in this chapter obtain. These conditions are, in short, the development of DME status with an incentive structure in which those who might demand quality HE – students, their parents, and employers – do not have sufficient incentives to do so. As a consequence, governments have little incentive to invest in this sector.

Romania has not been able to capitalize on the advantage of beginning transition with a relatively well-educated population. Instead, HE has stagnated or even declined, by some measures relative even to the communist period, by nearly all measures except for enrolment levels in international comparison. Given improved opportunities to study abroad, this leads to HE brain drain. At the same time, Romania has evolved into a DME in which there are limited domestic employment opportunities for the highly educated, who therefore face incentives to exit also after graduation. In this context, we can begin to explain the moderate level of quality of education provided by domestic universities by two factors operating in tandem: first, the weak incentives of students (and their parents) to care about quality education, given the lack of opportunities befitting a high skill level; second, low public priority for and spending on education given this demand structure (as well as other spending priorities, constraints of fiscal discipline, and a privatization drive). To complete the picture, Romania's European Union membership contributes to the reinforcement of dependency through improved access of students and highly skilled workers to the European common market. The most likely way out of the current equilibrium would be an evolution towards the liberal model (Hall and Soskice 2001), in which universities provide general skills and job training is achieved on the spot. But without a determined reprioritization of governmental regulatory effort and spending in favour of safeguarding HE quality, we see little hope for improvement in the quality of HE in Romania, nor in the country's ability to use improved qualification as a route to improved economic competitiveness.

Notes

1 This chapter is a revised and updated version of the article by Tarlea and Freyberg-Inan (2018), "The education skills trap in a dependent market economy: Romania's case in the 2000s", in *Communist and Post-Communist Studies, 51(1)*: 49–61.
2 We eschew the focus on vocational training which is appropriate for other contexts (Martin and Thelen 2007), as in Romania vocational training has all but disappeared since 1989.
3 The AHELO assessment is a feasibility study developed by the OECD meant to produce an equivalent to PISA for HE. However, results will only become available in 2020 and Romania has not taken part in the feasibility study.
4 Unfortunately, more recent figures are not available.
5 UNESCO data show that between 2000 and 2010, HE enrolment in Romania increased more strongly than in any other country in the world, except Cuba and Venezuela. Gross enrolment is measured as the number of students enrolled in a given level of education, regardless of age, expressed as a percentage of the official school-age population corresponding to the same level of education. For the tertiary level, the population used is the five-year age group starting from the official secondary school graduation (UNESCO 2017).
6 As explained previously, since 2010, enrolment in these private HE institutions has started to decrease.
7 Unfortunately, this data is patchy, not recent and includes private expenditures. Other reliable figures specifically for higher education or for different types of expenditure are not available, because Romania has failed to provide disaggregated data on education spending to Eurostat. According to unofficial data we obtained from Laurentiu Georgescu, an expert at the Bologna Secretariat (2011) in Bucharest, public higher education expenditure as a percentage of GDP was 0.45 in 2001, 0.44 in 2002, 0.43 in 2003, 0.45 in 2004, 0.46 in 2005, 0.63 in 2006, 0.85 in 2007, 0.75 in 2008, 0.59 in 2009 and 0.48 in 2010. These figures, unlike those from UNESCO, do not include private expenditures.
8 Public expenditure (current and capital) includes government spending on educational institutions (both public and private), education administration as well as subsidies for private entities (students' households and other private entities).
9 This was a widespread development in CEE. However, arguably HE in Romania has evolved more strongly towards the liberal market model than in Bulgaria, Poland or the Czech Republic (Dobbins 2011).

Appendix

This graphical representation of the production structure in Eastern Europe shows that agriculture maintains an important share of production in Romania, more important than in any of the other countries. Construction is also more important than in, e.g., Poland or Hungary. Overall, the primary and secondary sectors are more relevant in Romania than in other European countries.

Interviews conducted for this research:

Interviews were conducted between April 2011 and September 2012, predominantly in Bucharest and Sibiu. Two interviewees were re-contacted in December 2017. The selection of interviewees covers the most relevant actor categories: professors (engaged in academic activities in public and private universities), students and young employees as well as employees in HR departments or working in HR companies.

Universities:

- Interviewee U1. Lecturer, Alexandru Ioan Cuza University, Iasi. Kusadasi, Turkey, April 2012
- Interviewee U2. Pro-rector, Faculty of Petroleum-Gas University Ploiesti. Bucharest April 2012
- Interviewee U3. PhD candidate, Oxford University. Graduate of Babes-Bolyai University Cluj Napoca, March 2011
- Interviewee U4. Professor, University of Bucharest and (former) dean of the faculty of political science; member of the European Parliament. Bucharest, several interviews between April 2011 and September 2012
- Interviewee U5. Professor, Academy of Economic Studies, Faculty of Commerce, Chair of Tourism-Services. Academy of Economic Studies, Bucharest, September 7, 2011 and December 28, 2017
- Interviewee U6. Researcher, Institute for the Quality of Life, and lecturer, faculty of political science. University of Bucharest, September 5, 2012

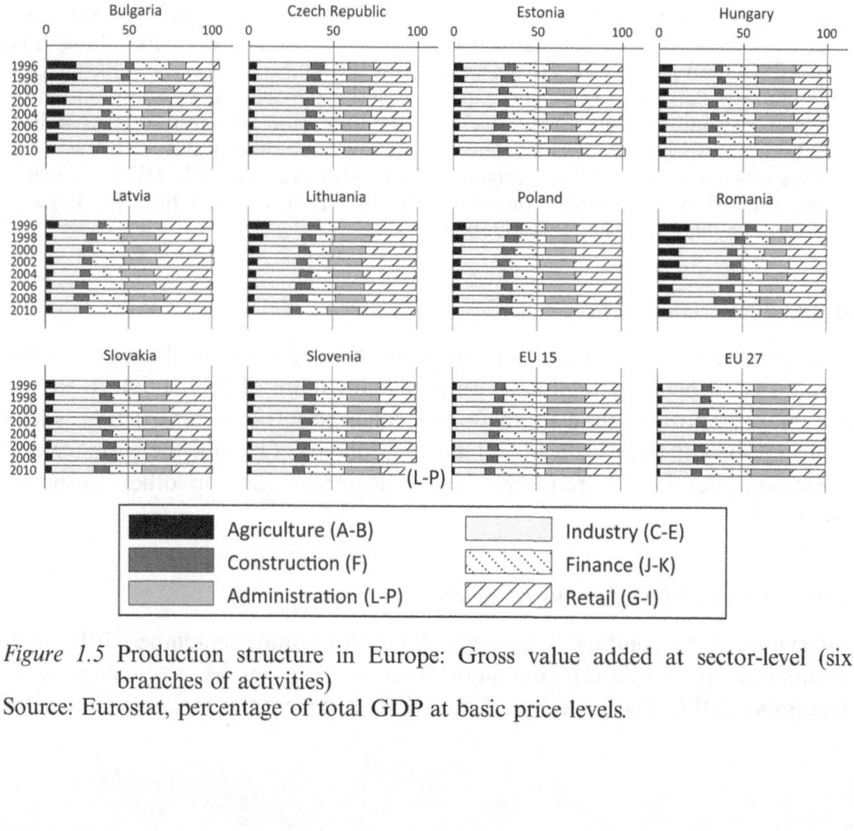

Figure 1.5 Production structure in Europe: Gross value added at sector-level (six branches of activities)
Source: Eurostat, percentage of total GDP at basic price levels.

- Interviewee U7. Associate Professor, Technical University of Cluj Napoca. Cambridge, UK, March 2012
- Interviewee U8. former head of the NSI (1996–1998), professor of statistics, Academy of Economic Studies. Bucharest, April 2011

Governmental institutions and non-governmental organizations:

- Interviewee N1. President Dinu Patriciu Foundation – NGO focusing on education in Romania. Bucharest, April 2011
- Interviewee N2. Head of department "Orizonturi Deschise", Dinu Patriciu Foundation. Bucharest, April 2011
- Interviewee N3. Head of the Bologna Secretariat in Bucharest 2010–2012. Several interviews and conversations in Bucharest between April 2011 and September 2012
- Interviewee N4. Programme director for educational initiatives, Romanian American Foundation. Bucharest, September 2012
- Interviewee N5. Expert, Bologna Secretariat Bucharest. Two interviews: April 2011 and March 2012
- Interviewee N6. EIU Services Manager; Senior consultant and researcher at Pythia International, Bucharest, April 2011
- Interviewee N7. Researcher, Institute for the Investigation of Communist Crimes and the Memory of the Romanian Exile. Bucharest, January 2012
- Interviewee N8. President, Group of Applied Economics (GEA), State Secretary Ministry of Finance 2012–2013. Bucharest, January 2012

Private companies:

- Interviewee P1. Human resources specialist, Banca Comerciala Romana. Bucharest, September 2011
- Interviewee P2. Junior Consult at Grayling. Bucharest, several interviews between January 2012 and September 2012
- Interviewee P3. HR manager resources, Continental Automotive Systems SRL Corporation, Sibiu. September 9, 2011 and December 29, 2017
- Interviewee P4. Catalyst Solutions, HR Manager. Bucharest, September 2011
- Interviewee P5. Account Executive, Saatchi & Saatchi. Bucharest. Several interviews between September 2011 and September 2012
- Interviewee P6. Oracle Corporation, HR specialist. Bucharest, September 2011

In addition, two **focus groups** with young employees and recent graduates were conducted in Bucharest and Sibiu in January 2012.

References

Agentia Romana pentru Asigurarea Calitatii in Invatamantul Superior (ARACIS) [The Romanian Agency for Quality Assurance in Higher Education] (2010)

"Barometrul calitatii 2010: Starea calitatii in invatamantul superior din Romania" [Quality barometer: Quality assurance in Romanian higher education.]. Available at: www.aracis.ro (Accessed: 28 December 2012).

Alexe, I. (2011) *Al patrulea val: Migratia creierelor romanesti pe ruta Romania-occident* [*The fourth wave: Brain Drain, Romania and the Western world*]. Bucharest: Soros Foundation.

Ansell, B.W. (2010) *From the ballot to the blackboard: The redistributive political economy of education*. New York: Cambridge University Press.

Bandelj, N. (2008) *From communists to foreign capitalists: The social foundations of foreign direct investment in postsocialist Europe*. Princeton, NJ: Princeton University Press.

Barro, R.J. and Lee, J.W. (2001) "International data on educational attainment: Updates and implications", *Oxford Economic Papers*, 53: 541–563.

Boeri, T. (2000) *Structural change, welfare systems, and labour reallocation: Lessons from the transition of formerly planned economies*. Oxford: Oxford University Press.

Bohle, D. and Greskovits, B. (2012) *Capitalist diversity on Europe's periphery*. Ithaca, NY: Cornell University Press.

Bologna Secretariat Bucharest (2011) Presentation on the Romanian education system.

British Council (2004) *Being young in Romania: Quantitative and qualitative survey*.

Campos, N.F. and Dabusinskas, A. (2002) "So many rocket scientists, so few marketing clerks: occupational mobility in times of rapid technological change", discussion paper. London: Centre for Economic Policy Research.

Chivu, L. (2009) "Romania: Multinational companies and collective bargaining", Institute of National Economy, Romanian Academy, European Industrial Relations Observatory paper RO0904049Q. Available at: www.eurofound.europa.eu/eiro/studies/tn0904049s/ro0904049q.htm (Accessed: 22 May 2013).

Deca, L. (2015a) "International norms in the reform of Romanian higher education: a discursive analysis", *European Journal of Higher Education*, 5(1): 34–48.

Deca, L. (2015b) "Challenges for Romanian higher education", *International Higher Education*, 82: 16–18.

Directorate general research and innovation 2011. Annual Report. Available at: https://ec.europa.eu/info/publications/annual-activity-report-2011-research-and-innovation-0_en (Accessed: 30 August 2018).

Dobbins, M. (2011) *Higher education policies in Central and Eastern Europe: Convergence towards a common model?* Basingstoke: Palgrave MacMillan.

Dobbins, M. and Knill, C. (2009) "Higher education policies in Central and Eastern Europe: Convergence toward a common model?" *Governance*, 22(3): 397–430.

Drahokoupil, J. (2009) *Globalization and the state in Central and Eastern Europe*. Abingdon: Routledge.

Economic Policy Committee and Directorate-General for Economic and Financial Affairs (2010) *Efficiency and effectiveness of public expenditure on tertiary education in the EU*, joint report. European Economy Occasional Papers 70, October. Brussels: EU Commission.

Epstein, R. (2014) "When do foreign banks cut and run? Evidence from west European bailouts and east European markets", *Review of International Political Economy*, 21(4): 847–877.

Ernst & Young – Raiffeissen Bank (2016) Barometrul antreprenoriatului romanesc. Available at: http://cursdeguvernare.ro/wp-content/uploads/2016/05/EY_Barometrul-antreprenoriatului-romanesc_2016_sinteza.pdf (Accessed: 15 January 2017).

European Bank for Reconstruction and Development (EBRD) – World Bank (2009) *Business environment and enterprise performance survey (BEEPS)*. Available at: www.ebrd.com/pages/research/economics/data/beeps.shtml (Accessed: 20 January 2013).

European Bank for Reconstruction and Development (EBRD) – World Bank (2017) *Business environment and enterprise performance survey (BEEPS)*. Available at: www.ebrd.com/pages/research/economics/data/beeps.shtml (Accessed: 20 January 2018).

Eurostat (2017) *Foreign affiliates statistics 2017*. Brussels: Eurostat.

Finegold, D. and Soskice, D. (1988) "The failure of training in Britain: Analysis and prescription", *Oxford Review of Economic Policy*, 4(3), 21–54.

Galbraith, K. (2003) "Towards quality private education in Central and Eastern Europe", *Higher Education in Europe*, 28(4): 539–558.

Goldin, C. and Katz, L. (2008) *The race between education and technology*. Cambridge, MA: Harvard University Press.

Graham, L.R. (1987) *Science, philosophy, and human behavior in the Soviet Union*. New York: Columbia University Press.

Hall, P. and Soskice, D. (eds.) (2001) *Varieties of capitalism: The institutional foundations of competitiveness*. Oxford: Oxford University Press.

Hanushek, E.A. and Wossmann, L. (2010) "Education and economic growth", in Peterson, P., Baker, E., and McGaw, B. (eds), *International Encyclopedia of Education*, 2: 245–252. Oxford: Elsevier.

Harvey, L. and Green, D. (1993) "Defining quality", *Assessment and Evaluation in Higher Education*, 18(1): 9–34.

Harvey, L. and Williams, J. (2010) "Fifteen years of quality in higher education", *Quality in Higher Education*, 16(1): 3–36.

International Monetary Fund (IMF) (2017) *World Economic Outlook 2017: World economic and financial surveys*. Washington, DC: International Monetary Fund.

Ives, B., Alama, M., Mosora, L.C., Mosora, M., Grosu-Radulescu, L., Clinciu, A.I., Cazan, A.M., Bădescu, G., Tufiş, C., Diaconu, M., and Duţu, A. (2017) "Patterns and predictors of academic dishonesty in Romanian university students", *Higher Education*, 74(5): 815–831.

Jones, E.A. and Ratcliff, J.L. (1999) "Global perspectives on program assessment and accreditation", in L. Lategan et al. (eds.), *Programme Assessment in Higher Education in South Africa*. Blomfontein, RSA: Unit for Higher Education Research, University of the Orange Free State.

Krueger, A. and Lindahl, M. (2001) "Education for growth: Why and for whom?", *Journal of Economic Literature*, 39: 1101–1136.

Marginson, P. and Meardi, G. (2009) "Multinational companies and collective bargaining", IRRU, University of Warwick European Industrial Relations Observatory paper TN0904049S. Available at: https://warwick.ac.uk/fac/soc/wbs/research/irru/wpir/wpir_103.pdf (Accessed: 30 August 2018).

Martin, C.J. and Thelen, K. (2007) "The state and coordinated capitalism: Contributions of the public sector to social solidarity in postindustrial societies", *World Politics*, 60(1): 1–36.

McMullen, M., Mauch, J.E., and Donnorummo, B. (2000) *The emerging markets and higher education*. New York: Routledge Falmer.

Mihai, A. (2011) "The businesses of private universities in Romania are worth 200 million euro yearly", *Ziarul Financiar*, September 10. Available at: www.zf.ro/profesii/200-de-milioane-de-euro-pe-an-businessul-universitatilor-private-din-romania-8718700 (Accessed: 10 September 2018).

Miroiu, A. and Aligica, D. (2008) *Public financing, fees and institutional structure and change in the Romanian higher education system*, Center for Economic Research and Graduate Education and the Economics Institute (CERGE-EI) Prague research paper. Available at: http://adrianmiroiu.files.wordpress.com/2008/03/public-financing-fees.pdf (Accessed: 14 November 2012).

Nicolescu, L. and Pun, C. (2007) "Relating higher education with the labour market: Graduates' expectations and employers' requirements", *Tertiary Education and Management*, 15(1): 17–33.

Nölke, A. and Vliegenthart, A. (2009) "Enlarging the varieties of capitalism: The emergence of dependent market economies in East Central Europe", *World Politics*, 61(4): 670–702.

Pop-Eleches, G. (2009) *From economic crisis to reform: IMF programs in Latin America and Eastern Europe*. Princeton, NJ: Princeton University Press.

Saldana, J. (2009) *The coding manual for qualitative researchers*. Thousand Oaks, CA: SAGE Publications.

St. Aubyn, M., Pina, A., Garcia, F., and Pais, J. (2009) "Study on the efficiency and effectiveness of public spending on tertiary education", *Economic Papers*, 390. Brussels: European Commission, Directorate-General for Economic and Financial Affairs.

Stark, D. and Bruszt, L. (1998) *Postsocialist pathways: Transforming politics and property in East Central Europe*. Cambridge: Cambridge University Press.

Tarlea, S. (2017) "Higher education governance in Central and Eastern Europe: A perspective on Hungary and Poland", *European Educational Research Journal*, 16 (5): 670–683.

Tomusk, V. (2000) "When East meets West: Decontextualizing the quality of east European higher education," *Quality in Higher Education*, 6(3) 175–185.

Tomusk, V. (2004) *The open world and closed societies: Essays on higher education policies "in transition"*. New York: Palgrave Macmillan.

UNESCO (2017) *UNESCO Institute for Statistics*. Available at: http://uis.unesco.org/ (Accessed: 30 August 2018).

van Vught, F. and Ziegele, F. (2012) *Multidimensional Ranking: The design and development of U-Multirank*. Dordrecht: Springer.

World Bank (2017) *World Development Indicators 2017*. Available at: https://data.worldbank.org/products/wdi (Accessed: 30 August 2018).

World Economic Forum (2017a) *Global Competitiveness Report 2017*. Available at: www.weforum.org/reports/the-global-competitiveness-report-2017-2018 (Accessed: 10 September 2018).

World Economic Forum (2017b) *Annual meeting*. Available at: www.weforum.org/events/world-economic-forum-annual-meeting-2017 (Accessed: 30 August 2018).

2 Multinational corporations and higher education

Some hidden dynamics

Introduction

One of the most dramatic dynamics in the new European Union member countries since 1989 has been the revolution in HE. It is surprising that these dynamics have remained largely unexplored in comparative politics, given the central role that governments play in regulating and financing HE. This chapter aims to fill this gap by presenting a straightforward argument formulated conceptually and tested empirically. It argues that three conditions needed to be satisfied in order for HE enrolment to increase. First, students are expected to want to enrol in universities; second, their skills need to be in demand in the market; and third, governments need to recognize the positive effects that the liberalization of HE would have on their popularity. However, two conditions can also suffice in order for enrolment to increase. Enrolment can increase without a real demand for high skills in these markets. This happens as long as the governments and the voters have incentives to offer and to demand high skills, respectively.

We present the puzzling developments in HE in the ten countries of Central and Eastern Europe (CEE). Enrolments have increased up to six-fold in some of these countries, while public and private funding of HE has largely lagged behind. However, we notice variation in the extent to which funding and enrolment diverge in the region. In turn, highly educated people have been absorbed into the economy, but economic growth has not been similarly spectacular. We unveil some of the channels that have led to these outcomes. In particular, it argues that this supply of skills, i.e. the increasing enrolments, can be explained by the atypical demand structure for *high* skills in these CEE markets. This structure has been shaped by the most relevant private employers in the market, multinational companies (MNCs), playing the crucial role on the demand side for high skills and governments playing the decision-making role on the supply side by liberalizing HE. Relying on data on firms collected by the European Bank for Reconstruction and Development (EBRD), it emerges that MNCs are more likely than domestic companies to employ HE graduates. These findings provide support for a model linking the development of HE to MNCs.

The interaction of three key players is analyzed: governments, MNCs as the key employers in these markets and students interested in working in MNCs. The way in which skills are used in the economy has influenced the spectacular enrolment levels and has in turn determined the different, but limited, economic growth trajectories in the region. The scope conditions of this theory are ideally fulfilled by the ten CEE post-communist European Union member countries. However, the set of countries that the theory applies to is not limited temporally or geographically. Ireland in the 1980s is a historical example, as well as contemporary events in other parts of the former communist bloc, including Croatia, Moldova or Serbia as well as in the south of Europe. The research question enquires into: *What explains the increasing enrolment in HE despite low funding? How can MNCs change incentives of individual voters and governments to adapt to certain level of skills?*

The employment scene for highly educated people has been fundamentally shaped by the entrance into these markets of foreign capital and of the MNCs that dominate employment demand in the region. The first section emphasizes the peculiarities of HE in the region and the increasingly dominant role of MNCs. It then situates this contribution in the relevant literature before presenting the argument in brief. We present macro-level data on inward foreign direct investment (FDI), on foreign affiliates statistics (FATS) and on the dynamics of HE indicators *enrolment* and *funding* in the ten CEE economies, showing their co-evolution. In the third section, aggregated empirical data on all these indicators is presented for the time-frame 2000–2012.[1] The model is presented in detail in the fourth section. These hypothesized relationships are also analyzed with firm-level data from the EBRD, before concluding.

1 Motivation and argument

It is surprising that HE has so far been forgotten in the political economy literature on the region despite its spectacular evolution and its crucial role in the political economies of these countries. HE is the level of instruction most likely to be conducive to an increase in the sophistication of economic activities and in subsequent economic growth, particularly in the CEE context in which vocational training has almost disappeared. Certainly, in the context of the fundamental changes taking place in CEE, academic interest materialized first in other burning issues, such as the complex and simultaneous processes of democratization and marketization (Blanchard 1997; Gehlbach 2008; Svejnar 1999, 2002), the formation of party systems (Stark and Bruszt 1998; Tucker 2006) and European integration (Hughes et al. 2002; Pop-Eleches 2008; Plümper et al. 2006). We argue that understanding the spectacular development of HE will provide more insights about important socio-economic developments in the region, most notably about the premises of these countries' ability to achieve economic growth through an increase in the sophistication of their economic activities.

Moreover, the evolution of HE is striking given that in this post-communist environment basic services, such as health or pensions, have deteriorated due to lack of funding, but HE seems to have fared particularly well. Enrolments have increased spectacularly and more students than ever from each cohort have been going to university in every country of our sample between 2006 and 2011. Enrolments have decreased slightly after 2011, marking an end to the expansion of private HE. What is most noteworthy is that the increasing enrolments took place despite the rather low levels of public funding for HE. Moreover, data on employment levels show that people with HE degrees are less likely to be unemployed than those without HE degrees. Unemployment levels have been systematically lower for highly educated people in the region. Table 2.4 in the Appendix shows differences between the unemployment levels of people educated at the upper secondary and post-secondary non-tertiary level – International Standard Classification of Education (ISCED) levels 3–4 – and the unemployment level of people with tertiary level education at ISCED levels 5–8. Unemployment has been half as high for highly educated people in 2015 – around 5 per cent across the region – compared to those people with only upper secondary education, where unemployment lay at 10 per cent across the region. Unemployment has been even higher for those with lowest levels of education. Nevertheless, it remains puzzling that the exploding enrolment in the HE market is not matched by equivalent economic growth in these countries. We therefore focus on *how skills are used* in these markets in which MNCs play an important role particularly in the realm of high-value-added activities.

The attempt to explain HE shifts attention to transnational actors – MNCs – which are able to influence the employment market. A large part of the dynamics in HE in terms of funding and enrolment can be linked to and partially explained by the role of MNCs. While the role of MNCs is significant, it does not explain all dynamics in HE. We argue here that MNCs can have a significant marginal effect on HE. The next chapters provide more context concerning *the links of MNCs to HE institutions.*

The role of MNCs after the fall of communism has been a topic of intense debate (Bandelj 2008; Bohle and Greskovits 2012; Drahokoupil 2008; Radosevic 2009). CEE countries, driven by a desire to upgrade their economies, have attracted FDI with varying consistency and success. Independently of the effects that MNCs have been shown to have in the countries of destination (Javorcik and Spatareanu 2008), the rhetoric of most post-communist governments has been in favour of foreign investment (Bandelj 2008). Only some politicians have started contesting the role of these MNCs. Viktor Orbán in Hungary after 2008, and the Law and Justice Party (PiS) in Poland since 2014 have been some of these contesters. The overwhelming support for MNCs is not surprising given their role as employers and as sources of capital. The extent to which an increase in the sophistication of these economies can be driven by FDI has drawn the attention of numerous studies (Görg and Strobl 2003; Liu 2008). The findings have been mixed and contingent on pre-existing domestic conditions in the destination countries of this foreign capital. We engage in this debate by exploring how skills determine and are in turn determined by the presence of MNCs, by focusing on the complementarities between providers and beneficiaries of HE.

2 Theoretical model

The peculiar evolution of HE in the post-communist context is a puzzling development that can best be defined in terms of three dimensions: (i) enrolments have increased despite low funding; (ii) the employment levels of people with HE degrees have continued to be higher than those of the population as a whole despite the booming number of HE degrees in the market (see Table 1 in Appendix); (iii) however, this up-skilling has not led to similarly spectacular economic growth. Given these three starting conditions, we contend that the reason for the modest economic growth in contrast to the rising educational achievement is explained by the way in which skills are used.

Given the complex mechanisms surrounding HE governance, the effects of MNCs on HE cannot be tested straightforwardly. Therefore, a model is proposed that hypothesizes that governments first seek foreign capital in an attempt to contribute to the capitalization of their markets. Equally, governments aim to create jobs, to increase the taxation base and to improve their economies. Historically, at the beginning of the transition in 1990, MNCs were not active in CEE, so they can be considered exogenous to the model. This means they did not influence government preferences in 1990 from *within* these countries. Secondly, international financial institutions and the governments of developed economies provided financial assistance and advice to CEE governments on the condition that state companies were privatized. Thirdly, given the extremely limited domestic capital accumulation and the idealized view of foreign capital (see Bandelj 2008), MNCs became the option of choice for governments in these countries.

In order to complete the argument, we also address the mechanisms through which MNCs influence HE when entering a new market and once they begin to be active in that market. Thinking about this counterfactually, an MNC would not relocate to a country if it could not find the required skills there, irrespective of whether the MNC's operations were inward-oriented or aimed at exporting goods or services. Likewise, a company would not be able to operate once having moved to a country if the necessary skills in the domestic market were not present or if it were not able to employ people from abroad. Therefore, the pre-existence of adequate skills is a necessary condition for an MNC to decide to invest or to continue operating in a given market. We push the argument further: *governments and MNCs barter skills.* Skills – high skills, such as those provided by universities – are crucial because they are able to attract foreign investment and will in turn determine the upgrading capacity of these economies. We present the theoretical argument in a more stylized version, as a game of strategic interaction.

3 Game of strategic interaction

3.1 Background information

MNCs have *a determining marginal effect* on the development of the HE system in CEE. Assuming rationality of the actors involved, the model explains that governments foster an increased enrolment in HE despite low funding, because the best opportunities for employment for graduates are MNCs. This partly explains the neglect of quality criteria (i.e. funding per student) in this process of HE enrolment expansion. Thus, the interaction between the government, the voter and the MNCs partly determines the increasing enrolment with no significant change in financing. In these CEE countries, the supply of skilled individuals is mostly assured by domestic universities. The behaviour modelled here is likely to lead to the best outcome for every actor involved. Lack of rationality and efficiency losses due to corruption are likely to lead to less efficient results.

The government has the prerogative to regulate HE. It can decide on the provision of HE in terms of two main dimensions, enrolment and funding, which are interdependent if the quality of HE is not to be compromised.[2] Further, spending on HE can stem from private and public sources. A consequence of the privatization of HE is that the government will not need to spend resources on additional enrolment. Liberalizing/privatizing HE can be used by governments to compensate lacking financial resources. Higher enrolment corresponds to the demand of voters and of employers (see Chapter 1 for a more detailed discussion).

Literature has shown that voters have different preferences for HE enrolment and funding depending on their socio-economic income group. Sophisticated models of voter preferences in HE are proposed by Ansell (2010) and Busemeyer and Iversen (2014). This influential work suggests that alliances can emerge between voters of different income quantiles: low, medium and high income. These groups are hypothesized to have different preferences concerning HE. The resulting alliances can support private or public HE, promoting models of elite or mass-level HE. We suggest that a less complicated mechanism is at play here, which stems from the peculiarities of the post-communist system.

The planned economy before 1989 would have provided every HE graduate with a graduate-level job. Voters expect that HE will be the key to white-collar employment independently of social background or gender. Hence, the median voter has a preference for access to HE, given the expectation that a degree will lead to a better job no matter how widespread these degrees are in the market. These insights have been drawn from semi-structured interviews with university professors and students (see Chapter 1 for more details).

Historically, during the very first stage of the transition, governments deregulated the HE markets and private HE institutions appeared. However, the imposed quality standards were lax, so the only optimization universities faced was profit maximization. The soft quality criteria could be explained as not only a strategic action by the government, but also as a consequence of the low administrative capacity of the state. No matter what factors better explain this outcome, the intensive margin (higher quality of HE) was ignored and only the extensive margin was considered. This implied high profit margins (revenues – costs). The main source of revenue was tuition fees and the main cost expenditure on staff, i.e. professors. Therefore, the maximization problem was simplistically reduced to maximizing student numbers relative to the number of professors in both private and public universities.

The way in which this equilibrium has arisen is at least partially explicable by the fact that the governments were not able to actively steer these processes at the beginning of the transition. This could have resulted from a combination of factors, including lack of bureaucratic capacity and corruption. Chapters 3 and 4 unveil how different actors, particularly governments, can contribute to breaking this vicious cycle. Here, we focus on the determinants of the relatively stable low-skills equilibrium.

Empirical support for the assumptions is presented in Chapters 1, 3 and 4 of the book. This model focuses on the key mechanism at work.

1 We assume that the government has a medium-run time framework for its policies. Hence, the government does not plan beyond more than two electoral cycles (four to eight years). In the long run, however, the government would earn a greater payoff from selling its labour force as a product of high-quality education, which would mean a higher payoff in a higher skill equilibrium.
2 We assume that the government gives fiscal incentives to FDI in a transition economy and, therefore, that taxes for MNCs are lower. Subsidies and taxes have been employed complementarily in CEE after 1990. Once offering subsidies was no longer an option because the countries belonged to the European common market and the countries needed to comply with European Union regulations, CEE governments have lowered taxes. Chapter 3 offers more insights on this.
3 We assume that MNCs will not have incentives to move to a CEE country and train its employees there in order to develop more sophisticated activities. MNCs will tend to move non-research-and-development (R&D) jobs in CEE countries. If R&D activities exist, they draw on the pre-existing skill pool. Therefore, voters are better off in a system with MNCs and poor-quality HE compared to a system in which MNCs require low skills but the students benefited from high-quality HE.[3] Voters' expectations would be higher after receiving high-quality HE, and these expectations would not be met in an economy dominated by MNCs. This would lead to an imbalance with the type of jobs MNCs have to offer.

We present here the extended-form game. We assume that there are three rational players: the government (G), the median voter (V) and the multinational corporation (M). The set of strategies are defined as follows:

The government chooses to offer or not to offer quality HE:

$$S_G = \{Q, NQ\}$$

The voter accepts or rejects this proposal, materialized as voting for the government which makes this offer or voting it out of office:

$$V_G = \{A, R\}$$

The MNC accepts and enters the market or rejects and does not enter (stays in its home country or invests elsewhere):

$$M_G = \{A, R\}$$

The payoffs are defined in utils. This means that they express the utility that each player receives in each scenario. The chosen values of the utilities are informative in relative terms, but meaningless in absolute terms. They represent the preferences of each of the players as these have been derived from interviews. In what follows I explain these relative relations between scenarios. I then show why NQ-A-A is a pure-strategy Nash equilibrium.

The three players choose strategies that maximize their payoffs.

3.2 The Voter

1 High percentage of high-skilled jobs AND a high tax to voter → voter rejects
2 High percentage of high-skilled jobs AND medium tax to MNC → voter accepts
3 Low percentage of high-skilled jobs AND low tax on MNC → voter accepts
4 Medium percentage of high-skilled jobs AND low tax on MNC → voter accepts

3.3 The MNC

1 High return from upgrade AND medium tax on MNC → MNC accepts
2 High return from upgrade AND high tax on MNC → MNC rejects
3 Low return from upgrade AND low tax on MNC → MNC accepts

Payoffs are defined in utils, which are hypothetically ordered values that each payoff receives, and they represent preferences of each of the actors:

QAA: G is satisfied (2), voter is satisfied (2), but not very satisfied because V is educated but unhappy with the job offered by the MNC, M is neutral (0)
QAR: G is unsatisfied (-8) (no MNC, but high costs of education), V is unsatisfied (-2) (no MNC, hence, no job), M is satisfied, goes elsewhere and is a little better off than if having to pay high wages (0)

QRA: G is satisfied (3) (it does not invest and it has MNCs), V is neutral (no quality but same jobs) (3), M is extremely satisfied (cheap labour force) (5)
QRR: G is unsatisfied (-2) (no MNCs), V is unsatisfied (-8) (no education, no MNC), M is satisfied (can go elsewhere)
NQAA=QAA
NQAR=QRR
NQRR=QAR

These payoffs represent the values for each choice that can be made by the actors. The high equilibrium implies high investment in skills, high demand of high skills and high productivity and the adaptation of each of the actors to this equilibrium. The low equilibrium implies low productivity and low investment. This is a baseline model and, as next chapters will show, there are differences between countries in terms of the sophistication level of activities. Some countries have been able to move to the right branch of the tree – the so-called virtuous branch – through strategic government interaction.

The tree is symmetrical. Not accepting quality equals accepting non-quality. This formulation implies that, controlling for everything else, the reasons why MNCs enter new markets in CEE is related to the kind of skills they find in the market. It explains *the marginal effect* of HE on the decisions of these three actors. It also argues that, once companies are active domestically, they will influence the production of certain types of skills and that the effect of MNCs on the domestic skill pool is virtually identical when entering the market and once being in the market.

This decision tree allows for an understanding of the political foundations of the determinants of HE in relation to requests from MNCs and vice versa. It explains the relevance of MNCs as employers of highly skilled individuals. It shows that the stable equilibrium that is reachable is one characterized by low- or medium-level skills. This is further explored in the empirical sections. This form of the game is simplified in order to be parsimonious. Further parameters can be added for determining the threshold at which the equilibrium moves from one branch of the tree to the other. This formulation is partisanship-blind. The following chapters show that government partisanship can matter on the margin even in the highly restricted space of manoeuvre of CEE.

3.4 Potential outcomes scenarios

Three alternative scenarios are considered. First, the scenario is considered in which MNCs do not enter these markets. Second, we consider the alternative in which the government increases the quality of HE, and, third, the options available to a voter with good quality HE are also spelled out. A first potential scenario is one in which MNCs do not enter the markets in CEE despite the efforts of governments to increase HE quality.

This would lead to a situation in which highly educated people would either (i) migrate, (ii) decide not to enrol at all or (iii) contribute in the long run to the development of domestic firms.

Putting this argument to the test, we could also ask: *What if the government decided to invest more in HE?* If the government was to increase education spending/student, this would lead to a better quality of education output. So, what are the premises that the government would deviate from the strategy outlined previously? First, the government would need to reduce the number of HE graduates, since it would be too expensive to produce an equally large number of degrees at a higher level of quality. Good quality could be obtained by cutting on enrolment, which is likely to be unpopular with voters. Second, this could increase the value of the labour force, which would eventually attract MNCs doing more sophisticated activities. We expect that this would make MNCs worse off: (i) the supply of people with degrees to choose from would be more limited; and (ii) it would increase their wage costs. Therefore, MNCs would choose other destinations to place their investment, which would make the government worse off by reducing its tax base and failing to attract more foreign capital. Therefore, the government will have in effect no incentive to deviate by offering good quality education given the assumptions. A government with a broader time-horizon would be willing to invest in HE, and this possibility is explored in Chapter 3 and Chapter 4.

Thinking about this counterfactually from the voter's perspective, one could argue that if the government offered good quality education, this would imply a deviation of the voter to better quality. If the voter's skills were not met in the domestic market, an over-qualified individual would be able to find employment to meet these skills abroad if the utility of working in a MNCs was smaller than the utility of working abroad. The capacity of these economies to retain talented people is judged to be very low according to surveys conducted by the World Economic Forum (WEF 2014). Also, more investment in HE could deter MNCs from entering these markets if it also led to higher taxes. Nevertheless, if this investment in HE was made, no matter the costs borne by the government in the short term, this could, at a later point, attract MNCs looking for a superior skill structure that was attained in the meantime.

4 Change in supply of HE in relation to demand for skills stemming from MNCs

The diagram in Figure 2.1 with the decision tree highlights the factors that influence skill formation once MNCs are active in a domestic economy as well as the moment it decides to move its location. Before proceeding with providing the mechanism of the argument, one further aspect needs to be clarified. This relates to the decisions of MNCs to relocate (to enter) or to remain in a given location (stay) once there. We argue here that these

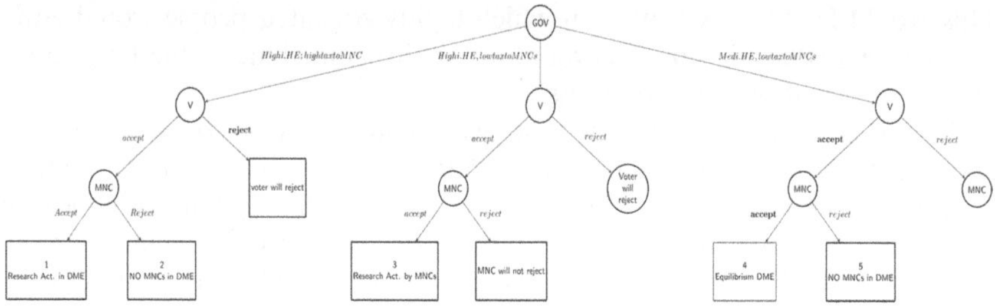

Figure 2.1 Decision tree for governments, voters, and multinational companies

decisions are essentially identical in their effect on HE and on the effect the existing pool of HE graduates has on their decisions. This formulation is agnostic regarding other factors that attract MNCs to a new economy. In the following, we show how the existing skills pool is likely to influence the decision of MNCs to enter domestic markets and will eventually also influence their evolution once there.

MNCs are significant employers across Europe, with corresponding influence in national collective bargaining systems due to their capacity to move production and jobs across borders (Eurofound 2009). Thus, MNCs have more room for manoeuvre than domestic companies (Eurofound 2009) and are more likely to implement their own strategies in a destination economy.

In the same way in which the prosperity of a city rests on the availability of skilled labour in that city (Glaeser 2011), we expect that the level of skills in a country will attract MNCs as well. We thus postulate that the argument holds for entire economies as well.

In the following, some formalization concerning the change in supply of HE depending on the demand stemming from MNCs is presented. We assume that the government has a facilitator role and it is thus not included in the model. We assume an equation for the supply of HE of the following shape:

$$HE_t^S = a_0 + b_0 HE_{MNC_t}^D$$

where HE_t^S represents the supply of HE at time t; $a_0$is the autonomous supply of HE (the MNCs supply of HE is 0); b_0 represents the magnitude of change in the supply of HE given one unit of change in the demand for HE.

We further decompose the MNCs' demand for HE.

$$HE_{MNC_t}^D = a_1 MNC_t$$

with MNC_t representing a measure of the number of MNCs at time t, and a_1 the magnitude of change in the demand for HE with a change in the number of MNCs. Further, MNC is written as:

$$MNC_t = a_2 MNC_{t-1} + b_2 HE^S_{t-1}$$

where MNC_t is the number of MNCs already established in the country; HE^S_{t-1} is the supply of HE at time $t-1$. a_2 represents the elasticity of MNCs (moving to the dependent market economy [DME] of interest) to world output, and b_2 is the magnitude of change in the number of MNCs given a one unit change in the level of HE supply existing in the previous year. After plugging (2) and (3) into (1) and computing the periodical change, the result is:

$$\frac{\Delta HE^s = a_1 a_2 b_0}{1 - a_1 b_0 b_2 \Delta MNC}$$

where $\frac{a_1 a_2 b_0}{1-a_1 b_0 b_2}$ is the multiplier that accounts for the between-countries variation.

The model thus formalized explains the influence of MNCs on the supply of HE. The equation explains that the supply of HE is determined by the presence of MNCs and, subsequently, MNCs determine the supply of HE.

Governments have played a central role in this process of expansion of HE by acting as facilitators. The most efficient way in which the government can reconcile these requests, i.e. attain this two-fold goal of increasing education and employment while continuing its own minimum investment, is by allowing enrolment in HE institutions to increase, i.e. through liberalizing this, and thus achieving its first goal. The higher share of highly educated people also attracts MNCs interested in employing these skilled people, allowing the government to also achieve its second goal. Given that both MNCs and students follow their own interests, the government only needs to liberalize HE and to use moderate resources for this purpose. This government strategy is also in accordance with the policy prescriptions of the World Bank and of the International Monetary Fund in the region during this time-frame.

At the same time, the increase in enrolment in HE institutions does not (always) accompany an increase in expenditure on education. The government does not need to increase spending for two reasons: students are willing to pay moderate tuition fees themselves, which has led to an intense privatization of the HE sector (as explained in Tarlea and Freyberg-Inan 2018) and, secondly, a government-funded competitive HE sector is not necessary to meet the demands for skills of MNCs. Companies are mostly attracted by the good skills-wage ratio and higher corporate taxes that could eventually be used for financing education. This interplay between the government and the MNCs explains the expansion of the HE sector with relatively little financing.

The evolution of HE, defined in terms of *enrolment* and *financing*, is a result of the way in which the government responds to requests from voters for two types of goods: *education* and *employment*. The liberalization of HE pursued eventually by all CEE governments was also a consequence of the Europeanization process in HE that affected both older and prospective

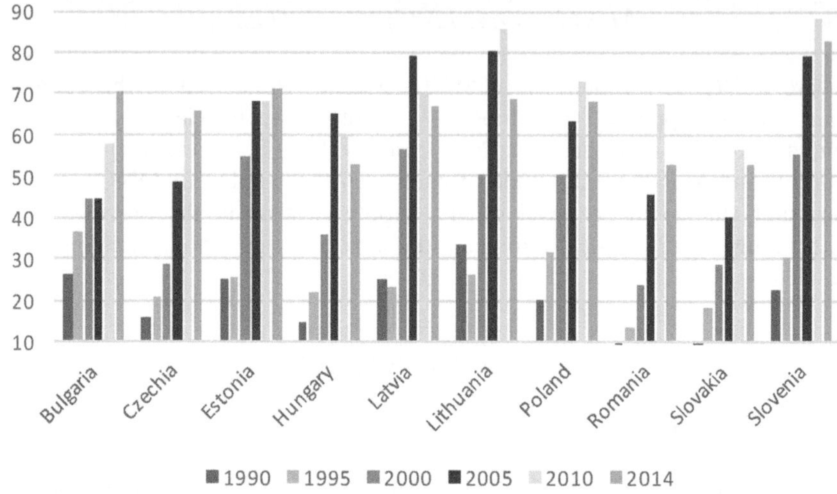

Figure 2.2 Gross enrolment ratio in higher education (percentage of a cohort)
Source: UNESCO 2017.

member countries of the European Union, as detailed by Dobbins (20011). At the same time, liberalization in HE corresponded to a world-wide privatization trend in HE.

4.1 Descriptive statistics on higher education enrolment and funding

An overview of the surprising HE dynamics and the increasing presence of foreign capital is presented in the next tables. The indicators on gross enrolment ratios in Figure 2.1 picture the increasing enrolment ratios in HE. The percentage of people attending university in each cohort after 1990 has increased tremendously.[4] We notice differences between countries as well. In Romania, enrolments have increased six-fold and in Hungary three-fold.[5] Participation increased between 1990 and 2010 from a regional average of less than 30 per cent of a cohort to around 70 per cent. Enrolments have stabilized or decreased slightly after 2010, which is also pictured in Figure 2.2. Moreover, the European Union supports improved educational attainment resting on the assumption that education will bear economic growth and well-being at both individual and aggregate levels (EU 2020). HE participation is expected to continue increasing,[6] which is also in line with the growing HE enrolments globally. However, the expectation that improved educational attainment would lead to economic growth has been only partially met in CEE.

We present other HE indicators in the next sections that are complementary to enrolment rates. First, we consider government spending on HE. This includes HE spending as a percentage of GDP and government expenditure as a percentage of general government expenditure. Subsequently, we consider data on private HE.

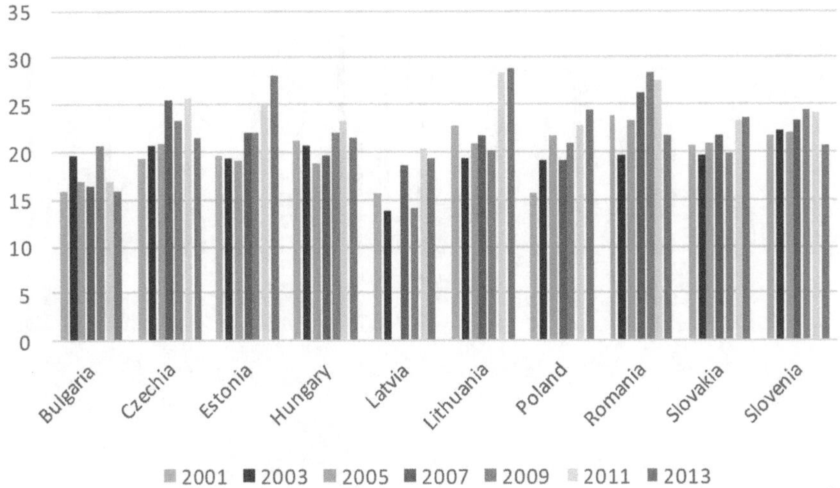

Figure 2.3 Higher education expenditure as a percentage of government expenditure
Source: UNESCO 2017.

We tackle variation in higher spending across the region that is pictured in Figure 2.3. The indicator public *expenditure on HE as a percentage of government expenditure* shows the government's commitment to investing in HE as compared to other public services. This indicator does not show a similarly upward trend as enrolment. Funding has evolved rather uniformly: in Latvia in 2001, spending on HE was 2.5 per cent of government expenditure; in 2010, it decreased to 2.2 per cent, while enrolments doubled. In Slovenia, it moved from 2.7 per cent to 2.8 per cent, while enrolment increased 2.5 times. This observed dynamic shows that governments have institutionalized the increase in HE enrolment but that state budgets have not borne the costs of this expansion.

Given that HE expenditure as a percentage of government expenditure is a relative measure, we also consider an alternative indicator. It could well be possible that the sizes of these governments budgets have increased and that HE expenditure higher relative to the GDP of the country could have gone up. This is not the case, as shown in Figure 2.4. Estonia, Lithuania and Slovenia spend most on HE, over 1.2 per cent of GDP.

Another alternative explanation for this outcome considered is that private HE has increased sufficiently to support enrolments. As Dobbins (2011) explains, the *privatization* of HE has taken place across the board in all countries and some students have borne the costs for HE themselves. Nevertheless, as data shows, these costs are moderate. Here, we notice some variation between countries. Data for the time-frame 1998–2015 in Figure 2.5 suggest that Latvia and Estonia have embraced the privatized form of HE, more so than the rest of the countries. The variation in enrolment in private HE institutions also reflects the differences in the management of education institutions. Estonia and Latvia stand out by registering very high enrolment

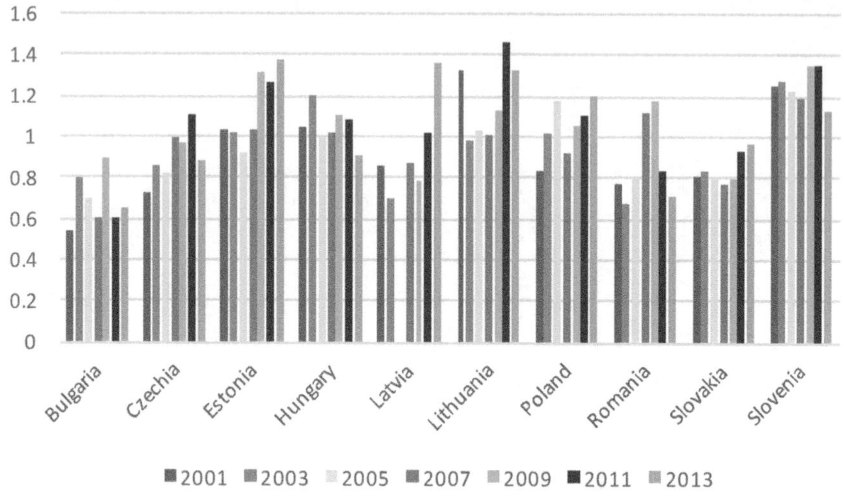

Figure 2.4 Government expenditure as a percentage of GDP
Source: UNESCO 2017.

rates in private HE institutions between 80 per cent and 90 per cent in private universities. Slovenia registered high enrolment rates until 2002, when enrolment rates started to drop. Poland and Romania had relatively high enrolment rates in private HE institutions, at 30 per cent, but these started decreasing after 2010. However, HE enrolment can be better understood in a relationship to the labour market. We turn in the following subsection to employment dynamics.

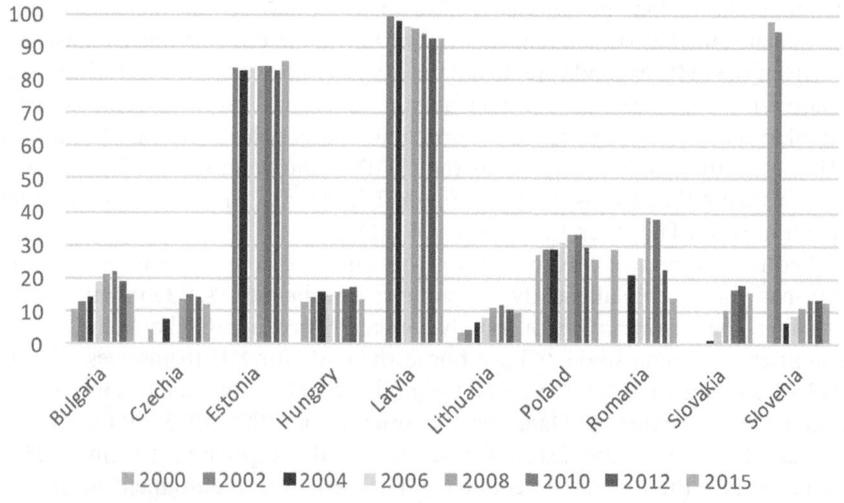

Figure 2.5 Percentage of enrolment in higher education in private institutions
Source: UNESCO 2017.

4.2 MNCs: employers and sources of capital

The *structural power of MNCs* stems from three sources that tend to reinforce one another. First, they are a key source of capital in these transition economies. Second, they are an important employment destination, and third, these companies are more likely to be innovative in transition economies compared to domestic companies (EBRD 2014). These three aspects underpin the structural power of MNCs and their ability to influence governments' and voters' preferences and actions. While voters and governments make decisions over investment in education, MNCs are an important link between them through the crucial role they play in the labour market.

MNCs have become a main source of capital, so their share in capital formation, as suggested by FDI data, is high. But, more importantly, their *structural role* shows that they are key private employers, as revealed by foreign affiliated statistics (FATS) data.[7] Data on *inward FDI* and on *inward FATS* [8] are suggestive of the role of MNCs in the CEE economies.

The FATS indicator provides insights into the economic impact of foreign investment in terms of job creation (FATS 2014). The indicator conveys information about diverse aspects of the activities of foreign-owned companies, such as share of employment or number of employees (Eurofound 2013). This data capture data on companies that are majority-owned by foreign entities and are thus more restrictive than the FDI indicator. FDI reflects the monetary value of foreign investments that exceed 10 per cent of the value of a company. Relying on FATS rather than on FDI allows us to measure the role of MNCs. FDI is much more inclusive. Table 2.2 shows that, on average, 20 per cent of employees in business employment between 2008 and 2010 have worked in MNCs.[9]

Further, we focus on the role of MNCs as employers in the CEE region. The indicator captures the number of people employed in business, i.e. industry, trade and services, excluding financial services. These are the sectors most likely to employ highly educated people and most likely to be engaged in economic activities leading to economic growth. In several countries in the sample, more than one-quarter of employees in productive services are employed by MNCs. Data in Table 2.1 shows that in Romania, approximately one million people out of the total of four million employees in private business employment were working in foreign-owned companies between 2008 and 2010. The Czech Republic, Romania, Hungary, Estonia and Slovakia have all had higher shares of their employees working in foreign-owned MNCs than the UK. In the Czech Republic, 27 per cent of employees were working in MNCs, compared to an average of 18 per cent between 2008 and 2010 in the UK.[10] The share of people working in MNCs is higher than in any other member country of the European Union, except for Luxembourg. The percentage of people employed in foreign-affiliated companies as a share of total business employment was calculated by relying on FATS and on Structural Business Statistics (SBS). In some CEE countries, the percentage of people working in MNCs is

Table 2.1 Percentage of business employment in MNCs

	2008	*2009*	*2010*
Bulgaria	13.1	-	13.7
Czech Republic	27.3	-	26.8
Estonia	22.4	22.3	22.5
Croatia		-	9.8
Latvia	15.6	17.1	17.3
Lithuania	12.4	13.9	14.2
Hungary	23.7	24.1	24.7
Poland	14.0	14.5	15.5
Romania	22.2	24.3	25.4
Slovenia	12.0	11.9	12.5
Slovakia	32.6	33.6	22.4

Source: FATS 2015.

higher than in the United States. MNCs are a major employer in these markets and can influence skill formation processes. Next chapter explains how foreign car manufacturers in Hungary collaborate with local universities and how the foreign-owned IT firms collaborate with local universities.

4.3 Foreign direct investment flows as per cent of GDP source: Eurostat

Further, we consider a complementary indicator on foreign investment: FDI. Figure 2.5 presents data on FDI flows as compared with GDP since governments are likely to be concerned by the importance of FDI flows in relation to yearly GDP figures. In order to explore how much bargaining power foreign investors have in these economies, we compare how much of what is registered to have been produced on a yearly basis (as a proportion of GDP) in an economy was produced by foreign companies. The indicator on FDI flows is more relevant than that on FDI stocks, given that we presume a short-term orientation of governments. Having data on the monetary value of these investment flows compared with the monetary value of the overall production in the economy is an indication of the relative importance of foreign investment. We present FDI data for a longer time-frame: 1990–2010. This can be found in Figure 2.6. In 2007, 30 per cent of GDP in Bulgaria was due to FDI inflows. More than 5 per cent of the GDPs of Estonia, Slovakia and the Czech Republic stemmed from FDI. Slovenia is the only country that stands out in this comparison, having the lowest levels of FDI. Moreover, Slovenia has registered the highest levels of outward FDI in the region. Here, FDI has started to increase since 2005. Another way to judge the relative importance of FDI flows is to consider that registering FDI inflows can influence whether a country registers economic growth that year.

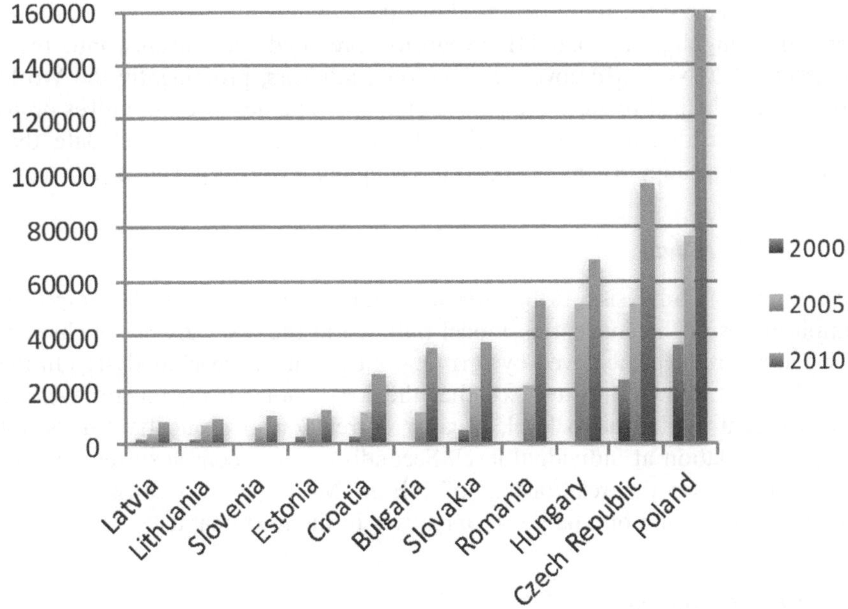

Figure 2.6 Foreign direct investment flows as percentage of GDP
Source: FATS 2015.

MNCs have thus gained structural power in CEE. As a consequence, they ought to also determine the choices of students and the evolution of HE. We need to note, however, that the prevalence of MNCs is not solely specific to the countries of CEE. MNCs play important roles in advanced capitalist systems as well. The Swedish and the UK economies register high levels of MNCs being active there. But one exceptional feature in CEE is that foreign MNCs prevail in terms of inward investment, whereas outward investment is almost absent. This large sector of inward FDI in comparison to an almost absent outward FDI sector is rather unique in the countries of CEE. Moreover, the most sophisticated activities tend to be concentrated in MNCs, which reinforce the dependency on MNCs and further underlines the importance of this relationship. This insight is generally known in policy circles. A report of the EBRD (2014) emphasizes the higher productivity of MNCs compared to the productivity in domestic companies.

All in all, these macro-level dynamics show a co-evolution of HE enrolment and employment in MNCs. But this co-evolution could be caused by various other factors than those outlined here. These dynamics are also the result of a general liberalization of these economies, which includes the opening of borders to foreign capital and the associated liberalization of the HE market. But the evolution of the HE market and of the labour market is intertwined. Understanding this connection also partially explains the relatively low – but not uniform across the region – investment in education. In the next comparative chapter, more details about the expansion of HE institutions are provided, highlighting that HE expansion preceded the entrance into these markets of MNCs. Moreover, international advisors, prominently the World Bank, have helped to steer these developments. The next section moves on to explain these dynamics at the micro level. We present firm-level data that provides some support for the conceptual model outlined previously.

4.4 Firm-level data

An empirical analysis at the firm-level underpins some of the empirical implications of the conceptual model outlined in the first part of the chapter. Two aims are to be achieved by carrying out this micro-level analysis. On the one hand, it allows us to test whether the correlations at the macro level are also present at the micro level, because correlation at group level does not imply correlation at individual level. Secondly, a more complex exercise is to ask whether we the relationship of HE to MNCs is also causal. This is achieved by relying on analytical narratives in the next chapter.

4.5 Data description

The data analyzed as follows was collected by the EBRD in its Business Environment and Enterprise Performance Survey (BEEPS). These surveys entailed the collection of cross-sectional data on companies from the ten countries of interest for this chapter and from other countries in CEE and Central Asia for the years 2002, 2005 and 2009. The EBRD surveys contain data on the same types of enterprise as do the data on foreign companies active domestically (FATS) and on all companies active domestically (SBS) provided by Eurostat, on which the first part of this chapter relies. The macro-level data is hence perfectly comparable to the micro-level data. BEEPS takes the form of face-to-face interviews with business owners and top managers. The surveys are administered by private contractors. BEEPS has been widely used for analyses of the business environment in these countries (Frye 2010 being one prominent example in political science literature).

The questions in the survey have evolved over its different rounds.[11] This means that quotas for the types of company – in terms of size, sector and ownership – have changed over time.[12] We also provide a snapshot from the 2009 survey. The 2009 data can be used to describe the population of interest as it is entirely representative of the population.

The survey from 2009 is representative for the non-agricultural private sector in these economies. Stratified random sampling was used in 2009, while quota (non-random) sampling was used in the previous rounds of the BEEPS. Thus, this paper uses probability weights in the analysis of the 2009 data. Aggregated data regarding the relevance of HE are presented in Figure 2.7. Since 2008, the survey universe has consisted of the majority of manufacturing sectors (excluding extraction), the retail and residual stratum that

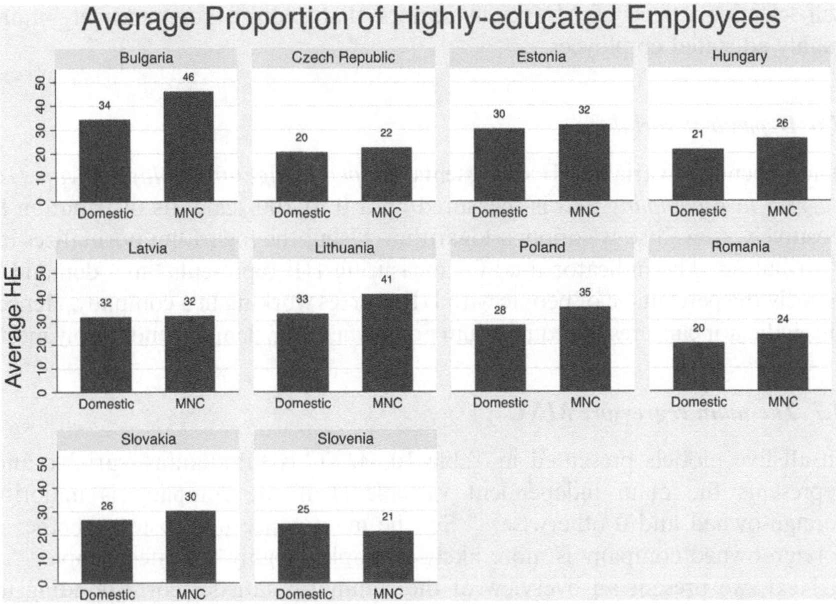

Figure 2.7 Percentage of employees with higher education degrees (firm-level)
Source: Descriptive statistics from the BEEPS survey in 2009 (EBRD – World Bank 2017).

includes most service sectors (wholesale, hotels, restaurants, transport, storage, communications, IT) and construction.[13]

Figure 2.7, with data from 2009, distinguishes between the proportion of employees with HE degrees in MNCs and the equivalent proportion in domestic firms. On average, MNCs employ more staff with HE degrees than domestically-owned companies. But BEEPS data also show that domestically-owned companies are more numerous than foreign-owned ones. We notice that a higher proportion of highly educated people work in MNCs in contrast to domestically-owned ones. The only exception is Slovenia, with a smaller proportion of highly educated employees in MNCs in comparison to domestically-owned companies. At the same time, Slovenia also registered outward MNCs, being active particularly in the former Yugoslavian countries. Differences across countries are explored further in the next chapter.

The sector breakdown was carried out in accordance with International Standard Industrial Classification (ISIC) codes, as follows: manufacturing (1000/3499), construction utility (3500/4399 and 6800/6899), retail (4400/5799), IT and finance (5800/6699), professional and administrative (6900/8299), other (8400/9900 and 0/1000). IT and finance does not include the banking sector (which is more than 80 per cent foreign-owned in every country), because this is subject to government regulation and does not meet the BEEPS criteria. The firm-level regression analysis uses a five-point category for ISIC. This variable is used with the aim of controlling for a self-selection effect of MNCs in sectors that require comparatively more highly educated employees.

4.6 Dependent variable

The dependent variable HE represents *the percentage of employees with HE degrees in a company* and is measured on a 0 to 100 scale. Its distribution is positively skewed so we apply a logarithm. Using the logarithm normalizes its distribution. The indicator used for measuring HE represents "met demand", namely the percentage of people with HE degrees working in a company. Hence, this indicator captures the equilibrium point where HE demand and supply meet.

4.7 The main regressor: MNC

In all five models presented in Table 10, *MNC* is the dummy variable and represents the main independent variable (1 if the company is majority foreign-owned and 0 otherwise).[14] So, the main concern is to test whether a foreign-owned company is more likely to employ highly educated people.

Next, we present an overview of the summary statistics corresponding to the variables we hypothesize to be relevant in our model (see Table 2.2).

4.8 Do highly educated people work in MNCs?

We are interested in which companies active domestically employ people with HE degrees. This would allow us to identify the relevant employment destinations for highly skilled individuals. The results show (see table estimation) that

Table 2.2 Summary statistics

Variable	*Mean*	*Standard deviation*	*Minimum*	*Maximum*	*N (number of observations)*
Proportion of employees with HE degrees	21.88	26.35	0	100	8,600
Multinational company	0.11	0.32	0	1	8,600
Industrial classification (5 categories)	1.96	1.02	1	5	8,521
Company size	1.73	0.79	1	3	8,592
Research and development	0.24	0.47	0	2	9,270
Quality assurance	0.21	0.41	0	1	9,186
Exporting company	0.09	0.28	0	1	9,270

MNCs are more likely than domestic companies to employ HE graduates. The estimation of the (met) demand for HE degrees is operationalized in several steps – using basic statistical models. We estimate met demand (where supply and demand meet) given that the survey does not distinguish between who employers would like to employ and who they are able to employ.

A preliminary analysis shows that the differences in means between MNC and non-MNC in terms of employment of highly educated people are statistically different from zero. We use country-fixed effects in order to control for all the intrinsic country-specific characteristics of the business environments and estimate difference in means again in Model 1. Models 2, 3 and 4 use ordinary least squares (OLS) with country-specific fixed effects to explain within-country variation. Therefore, controlling for macro-level characteristics is no longer needed. We only control for firm characteristics in Model 2 and pool all the years. Given that questions have changed during the different rounds of the survey and that, hence, not all sectors are included in the same way each year, it makes sense to also analyze the data using year dummies (Model 3 in Table 2.3 – only with data from 2009). These analyses show that being MNCs correlates with a higher percentage of employees with HE degrees.

The estimated coefficient on our main-interest dummy-variable MNC comes with a positive sign throughout all models specified. While we display all specifications, we realize that a simple least squares bivariate regression will omit many variables of interest, giving our estimation a large upward bias. Once we control for size of firm, type of industry, country of origin and population of the city where the firm is located, the magnitude is reduced. A MNC tends to employ around 10 per cent more staff with HE degrees than its domestic counterpart. However, these are imperfect measures of the dynamics between MNCs and educational attainment, and we therefore refrain from drawing policy implications.

4.9 Other firm-level controls

Certain economic activities are more likely to demand high skills than others. Moreover, MNCs do not choose their areas of activity randomly. The regression controls for the *industry-specific sector*, which should clarify whether MNCs are more skill-intensive. Hence also, including this control clarifies whether, within a given sector of economic activity, a MNC is more likely to employ HE graduates than is a domestic company. Data in Regression Table 2.3 shows that the effects are significant both statistically and substantially. Companies active in administration are more likely to employ highly education individuals than companies in industry. Similarly, companies in retail are more likely to employ HE individuals as well.

The size of the company is also expected to influence the percentage of people with HE degrees within a company. Large companies tend to employ fewer highly educated people as a proportion of their staff. This finding is not surprising, given the level of sophistication of firms in these economies. Large

Table 2.3 Regression results

Dependent variable: proportion of highly educated employees in a company	*(1) Country fixed effects*	*(2) Country fixed effects*	*(3) Country fixed effects*	*(4) Country-year fixed effects*
Multinational companies (MNCs)	8.43*** (0.94)	10.30*** (0.92)	3.21* (1.30)	8.91***
Retail sector	–	5.27*** (0.57)	1.30 (0.82)	5.10*** (0.57)
IT-finance sector	–	6.04*** (1.10)	-0.04 (1.54)	4.89***
Administrative sector	–	32.38*** (1.31)	30.75*** (4.70)	29.07*** (1.33)
Other activity sector	–	18.84*** (1.92)	14.09 (9.30)	16.25*** (1.90)
Size of the company	–	-4.48*** (0.36)	-2.13*** (0.57)	-4.84*** (0.35)
Research and development activities	–	2.47*** (0.57)	3.04*** (0.72)	2.97*** (0.57)
Quality assurance	–	3.59*** (0.62)	5.08*** (0.92)	5.18*** (0.62)
Exporting company	–	1.12 (0.93)	-1.32 (1.12)	1.11 (0.91)
City: larger than 1 million people	–	–	-11.52** (2.79)	–
City: 250,000–1 million people	–	–	-2.92 (1.88)	–
City: 50,000–250,000 people	–	–	-8.77*** (1.30)	–
City: less than 50,000 people	–	–	-12.77** (1.14)	–
2005	–	–	–	-8.26*** (0.76)
2009	–	–	–	-13.22** (0.75)
Constant	20.94*** (0.64)	21.78*** (0.87)	25.85*** (1.97)	30.26*** (1.88)
Observations	8600	8431	2797	8431
Adjusted R sq.	0.05	0.17	0.17	0.20

Note: Standard errors in parentheses *p <0.05, **p <0.01, ***p <0.001.

companies are not expected to be focusing on research and development or, consequently, to have a large share of highly skilled workforce. *The sophistication level of a company* will also determine its likelihood in employing people with HE degrees. We use the existence of quality certification (ISO) and of research and development (R&D) activities within the company as proxies for sophistication, following Commander and Kollo (2008).

Exporting companies are expected to be competitive in international markets and therefore be more likely to employ highly educated people. However, our analysis shows that the coefficient is insignificant and sometimes even negative. So, exporting companies tend to employ fewer people with HE degrees, or this effect is insignificant. This seems counter-intuitive. But this argument is supportive of the DME model. Exporting companies are not necessarily producing sophisticated products. On the contrary, on average, exporting companies do not hire more people with HE degrees than non-exporting companies, controlling for everything else. Indeed, the sophistication level of exports is closer to the raw materials category than to sophisticated goods. Further supportive of this, Bohle and Greskovits (2012) refer to these companies to be "the sweatshops of Europe", i.e. exporting assembled goods to western Europe. Both exporting goods close to raw materials in terms of manufacturing stage as well as assembling goods requires little sophistication.

The regressions also control for *regional differences*. Inspired by the work of Glaeser and Resseger (2010) and Glaeser (2011), we expect companies that are active in larger cities to employ a higher proportion of people with HE degrees than those active in rural areas or in smaller cities. We find this to be the case. Companies employing people with HE degrees tend to be concentrated in larger cities. The reference category is the capital city; hence, the coefficient for the smaller cities is negative. Once we control for the size of the city, the coefficient for MNC also decreases, which shows that MNCs tend to concentrate in larger cities.

All in all, this empirical exercise shows that, in CEE, a higher proportion of highly educated individuals tend to work in MNCs compared to domestically-owned companies. This provides empirical support for the argument that the evolution of HE in the region ought to be understood in relation to MNCs. But most intriguingly, the empirics speak to the structural relevance of MNCs in CEE.

An alternative way to cross-validate the argument about the relationship between MNCs and the evolution of HE is to test whether highly educated people are absorbed into the labour market. If unemployment levels amongst highly educated people are largely similar or higher than amongst uneducated people, then it would be difficult to sustain the argument. But this is not the case. Unemployment levels among educated people have been lower than the general unemployment levels during this time-frame (see Figure 2.8). This should not come as a surprise, as educated people are expected to be more flexible in the labour market and, hence, more employable (Svenjar 1999 offers a comprehensive overview).

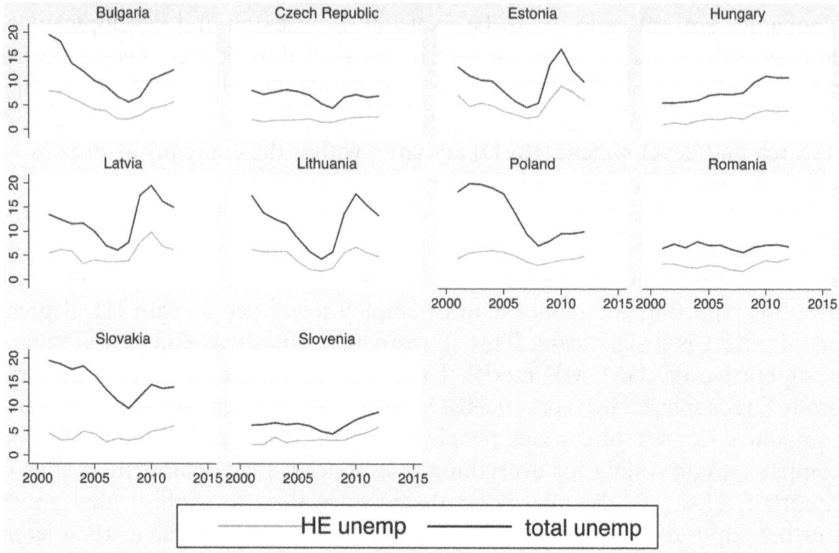

Figure 2.8 Unemployment levels by level of education; total unemployment versus unemployment of highly-educated people
Source: FATS 2015.

Conclusions

This chapter has started by arguing that governments in CEE ought to be responsive to the expectations of MNCs when regulating HE. Moreover, the relationship between MNCs and HE institutions can be mediated by voters. We presented a mechanism meant to explain how the presence of MNCs has influenced the evolution of the HE sector in CEE and vice versa. MNCs have significant structural power in CEE by being both an important source of capital and one of general employment. MNCs are key employers of highly educated individuals, as firm-level statistics show. They can influence the demand for labour in these countries. Subsequently, one consequence identified and tackled in this chapter has been the inability of these countries to improve the quality of their HE given the interdependencies that exist between employers, voters and governments in power. The intuition of the argument is straightforward: economies dependent unilaterally on foreign capital also build other ties to these MNCs, and these ties are difficult to influence by a government, particularly by a government with a narrow time horizon. MNCs end up determining the incentives structures in the entire economy, including the incentives of students and governments and ultimately the development of the HE system.

In particular, it is argued that the governments in each of these countries have played a central role in facilitating the *supply* and *demand* of skills. Governments have enabled an increasing role for foreign firms – MNCs – that demand HE degrees. The demand of MNCs for relatively low to averagely high skills at least partially explains the supply of HE. In a first step, the government responds to popular demand for the liberalization of HE and allows the supply of HE to meet the demand in a free-market-economy spirit. Similarly, MNCs find the skills resulting from this equilibrium to be a suitable resource for their businesses. They thus contribute to a self-sustainable dynamic. Neither the MNCs nor the government on their own would have been able to influence this outcome. The coexistence of these two institutions chasing their own interests has led to this outcome.

The chapter relies on data rarely used so far for research on foreign companies in CEE: both FDI and FATS statistics. Furthermore, Nölke and Vliegenthart (2009) do not characterize Romania or Bulgaria to be particularly dependent on FDI. But if relying on FATS statistics, it is precisely these two countries, more than any other in the sample, that depend on foreign companies for employment. This further underlines the importance of relying as precise as possible on indicators for depicting the processes of interest. For this purpose, the chapter provides individual-level mechanisms and predictions to explain these macro-level phenomena. But this presented model is also surrounded by noise. Hence, the relationships described do not and need not follow this model smoothly. The model explains the links between these complex phenomena and is distinguishable from those accounts of HE evolution as an essentially chaotic phenomenon.

A key implication of these findings is that governments need to spend more on HE and at the same time bargain with MNCs to move production activities to their countries that require more sophisticated labour. Next chapter shows how some governments in Hungary and Poland have managed to make these improvements simultaneously.

Notes

1 Reliable comparable data is not available for the time-frame 1990–1999. This limitation is not worrisome, given that these countries' commitment to developing as market economies and as democracies became less questionable after the year 2000.

2 We assume the economy of scale will not make a supplementary HE degree less costly.

3 Voters and students are considered synonymously.

4 Gross enrolment ratios account for differences between cohort sizes by representing "the total enrolment within a country in a specific level of education, regardless of age, expressed as a percentage of the population in the official age group corresponding to this level of education" (UNESCO 2017).

5 Gross enrolment ratios are a conservative indicator for HE increase given the large sizes of cohorts that came of age during this period (people born in the 1980s).

6 According to the Lisbon Agenda, the share of the population aged 25 to 64 who have completed tertiary education should reach at least 40 per cent by 2020. The current tertiary education attainment of people aged 25 to 64 years is less than 30 per cent in all the ten countries studied (Eurostat 2015).

7 Multinational companies (MNCs) are used synonymously to transnational companies (TNCs), and these are defined, in accordance with the data from FATS, as more than 50 per cent foreign-owned.

8 Outward FDI and outward FATS are extremely low in these ten countries and, hence, not of interest.
9 Perfectly comparable data on both SBS and FATS is not available after 2010.
10 These figures exclude companies that are less than 50 per cent foreign-owned.
11 As such, the data collected since 2008 has been incorporated into the enterprise surveys conducted by the World Bank in other parts of the world.
12 Before 2008, there were three levels of stratification: industry, size and region. In 2002, quotas were used for sector, size (number of employees), location and ownership quotas (foreign and state-owned). Exporter quotas were added for the 2005 round. The survey universe consisted for the 2002 and 2005 rounds of industry and most service sectors. Firms that operated in sectors subject to government regulation, such as banking, electric power, rail transport and water and waste water, were excluded. Only formal (registered) companies with two or more employees and at least three years old were eligible for interview. There were no restrictions on ownership.
13 Only registered companies with five or more employees are eligible for interview. Firms in 100 per cent government (state) ownership are not eligible to participate in BEEPS. The sampling frame is derived from the universe of eligible firms obtained from the country's statistical office. The strata for BEEPS are firm size, sector and geographic region within a country. Firm-size levels are 5–19 (small), 20–99 (medium) and 100+ employees (large). Sector breakdown is usually into manufacturing, retail and other services.
14 The variable was coded in order to distinguish companies that are more than 50 per cent owned by a foreign entity. This is consistent with the operationalization of Eurostat and used as such in foreign affiliates statistics (FATS).

Appendix

Table 2.4 Unemployment rates by educational attainment (%)

Country/ year	*2000 (ISCED 3–4)*	*2000 (ISCED 5–8)*	*2000 (ISCED 3–4)*	*2010 (ISCED 5–8)*	*2015 (ISCED 3–4)*	*2015 (ISCED 5–8)*
Bulgaria	15.8	6.7	9.7	4.6	8.3	4.0
Czech Republic	7.8	3.0	6.9	2.8	4.7	2.4
Estonia	15.0	5.1	19.1	9.4	6.8	3.9
Latvia	14.8	7.2	21.1	10.6	10.8	4.9
Lithuania	20.2	9.3	21.8	7.7	11.7	3.7
Hungary	6.4	1.4	10.6	4.6	6.4	2.4
Poland	17.0	5.5	10.5	5.0	8.4	4.0
Romania	9.4	3.6	8.0	4.8	7.2	4.1
Slovenia	6.9	2.2	7.5	4.3	9.9	5.8
Slovakia	18.4	5.3	14.1	5.8	10.9	6.0

Source: Eurostat 2017.

Note: ISCED 3–4 includes upper secondary education and post-secondary non-tertiary education. ISCED 5–8 includes tertiary education.

References

Ansell, B. (2010) *From the ballot to the blackboard: The redistributive political economy of education*. Cambridge, MA: Cambridge University Press.

Bandelj, N. (2008) *From communists to foreign capitalists: The social foundations of foreign direct investment in postsocialist Europe*. Princeton, NJ: Princeton University Press.

Blanchard, O. (1997) *The economics of post-communist transition*. Oxford: Clarendon Press.

Bohle, D. and Greskovits, B. (2012) *Capitalist diversity on Europe's periphery*. Ithaca, NY: Cornell University Press.

Busemeyer, M.R. and Iversen, T. (2014) "The politics of opting out: explaining educational financing and popular support for public spending", *Socio-Economic Review*, 12(2): 299–328.

Commander, S. and Kollo, J. (2008) "The changing demand for skills Evidence from the transition", *Economics of Transition*, 16(2): 199–221.

Dobbins, M. (2011) *Higher education policies in Central and Eastern Europe: Convergence towards a common model?* Berlin: Springer.

Drahokoupil, J. (2008) *Globalization and the state in Central and Eastern Europe: The politics of foreign direct investment*. Abingdon: Routledge.

EBRD – World Bank (2017) *Business environment and enterprise performance survey (BEEPS)*. Available at: www.ebrd.com/pages/research/economics/data/beeps.shtml (Accessed 20 January 2018).

Eurofound (2009) *Multinational companies and collective bargaining*. Dublin: European Foundation for the improvement of living and working conditions. Available at: www.eurofound.europa.eu/sites/default/files/ef_files/docs/eiro/tn0904049s/tn0904049s.pdf (Accessed: 10 September 2018).

European Bank for Reconstruction and Development (EBRD) (2014) *European Bank for Reconstruction and Development: Annual indicators*. Available at: www.ebrd.com/what-we-do/economic-research-and-data/data/forecasts-macro-data-transitionindicators.html (Accessed: 14 November 2016).

Eurostat (2017) *Unemployment rates by educational attainment*. Available at: https://ec.europa.eu/eurostat/web/products-datasets/product?code=tepsr_wc140 (Accessed 13 September 2018).

FATS (2014) *Foreign Affiliates*. Brussels: Eurostat.

Frye, T. (2010) *Building states and markets after communism: The perils of polarized democracy*. New York: Cambridge University Press.

Gehlbach, S. (2008) *Representation through taxation*. New York: Cambridge University Press.

Glaeser, E. (2011) *Triumph of the city: How our greatest invention makes US richer, smarter, greener, healthier and happier*. Basingstone: Pan Macmillan.

Glaeser, E.L. and Resseger, M.G. (2010). "The complementarity between cities and skills", *Journal of Regional Science*, 50(1): 221–244.

Görg, H. and Strobl, E. (2003) "Multinational companies, technology spillovers and plant survival", *The Scandinavian Journal of Economics*, 105(4): 581–595.

Hughes, J., Sasse, G., and Gordon, C. (2002) "Saying 'maybe' to the return to Europe: Elites and the political space for Euroscepticism in Central and Eastern Europe", *European Union Politics*, 3(3): 327–355.

Javorcik, B.S. and Spatareanu, M. (2008) "To share or not to share: Does local participation matter for spillovers from foreign direct investment?" *Journal of Development Economics*, 85(1): 194–217.
Liu, Z. (2008) "Foreign direct investment and technology spillovers: Theory and evidence", *Journal of Development Economics*, 85(1): 176–193.
Nölke, A. and Vliegenthart, A. (2009) "Enlarging the varieties of capitalism: The emergence of dependent market economies in East Central Europe", *World Politics*, 61(4): 670–702.
Plümper, T., Schneider, C., and Troeger, V. (2006) "The politics of EU eastern enlargement: Evidence from a heckman selection model", *British Journal of Political Science*, 36(1): 17–38.
Pop-Eleches, G. (2008) *From economic crisis to reform: IMF programs in Latin America and Eastern Europe*. Princeton, NJ: Princeton University Press.
Radosevic, S. (2009) "Research and development, competitiveness and European integration of south eastern Europe", *Europe-Asia Studies*, 61(4): 621–650.
Stark, D. and Bruszt, L. (1998) *Postsocialist pathways: Transforming politics and property in East Central Europe*. Cambridge: Cambridge University Press.
Svejnar, J. (1999) "Labor markets in the transitional central and east European economies", *Handbook of Labor Economics*, 3: 2809–2857.
Svejnar, J. (2002) "Transition economies: Performance and challenges", *Journal of Economic Perspectives*, 16(1): 3–28.
Tarlea, S. and Freyberg-Inan, A. (2018) "The education skills trap in a dependent market economy: Romania's case in the 2000s", *Communist and Post-Communist Studies*, 51(1): 49–61.
Tucker, J.A. (2006) *Regional economic voting: Russia, Poland, Hungary, Slovakia, and the Czech Republic, 1990–1999*. Cambridge: Cambridge University Press.
UNESCO (2017) *UNESCO institute for statistics 2017*. Available at: http://uis.unesco.org/ (Accessed 30 August 2018).
World Economic Forum (WEF) (2012) *Global competitiveness report 2012/2013*. Technical report no. 196. Geneva: World Economic Forum.

3 Higher education governance in Central and Eastern Europe[1]

A perspective on Hungary and Poland

Introduction

This chapter seeks to answer the question of what motivates governments to introduce and implement reforms in higher education (HE). The political and economic reasons why some governments in the countries of Central and Eastern Europe (CEE), for the period 1990 and 2015, have invested resources in order to facilitate cooperation between employers and universities and have introduced quality criteria in HE finance while others have not are identified. Use of a comparative perspective on Poland and Hungary revealed important differences in HE regulations in these seemingly otherwise very similar cases, showing that what drives regulations, at least in part, is the governments' responses to the labour market, i.e. the dynamic between students – future workers – and employers – largely multinational companies (MNCs). Moreover, differences in HE regulations in the two countries are responsive to voters' concerns. The chapter thus contributes to the literature on skill formation in CEE and to the literature on political economy focusing on this part of the world.

Why have different models of HE governance emerged in the countries of CEE? Two contrasting models of HE governance have developed in Hungary and in Poland in the first 25 years following the collapse there of communism. This difference is puzzling given the many similar features of the two countries. This chapter explains the emergence and the evolution of these two contrasting models of HE governance and argues that political parties in government have been driven by political motivations when regulating HE. Rather than focusing on the administrative and financial capacity of the government, the focus here lies on the motivations of governments to pursue such reforms. As such, this provides a political-economic perspective by concentrating on the incentives of governments to act. Polish and Hungarian governments have designed reforms aimed at incentivizing businesses and students to invest in skills provided by universities in different ways. These governments sought to build and improve a relationship between employers and universities and introduced quality criteria in the funding mechanism of HE. However, the ways in which the reforms have taken place show significant variations between and within countries. The set of constraints that make the reform of HE – aimed at improving its fitness for purpose and, thus, its quality and labour market suitability – uncomplicated has led to different HE models in Hungary and in Poland. These different HE models mirror different coordination mechanisms in these economies. Signs of coordination emerged in Hungary – a more liberal regime developed in Poland.

The point of departure of this study is represented by existing theories about comparative capitalism in the region (Bohle and Greskovits 2012; Nölke and Vliegenthart 2009) as well as analyses of HE governance (Busemeyer and Trampusch 2011; Dobbins 2011; Kwiek 2012). This chapter interprets these HE reforms in a new theoretical framework by showing that the institutional determinants of HE governance are more complex than has previously been shown. This is one of the first studies about the political economy of human capital formation in post-communist CEE. The chapter also considers Romania as a shadow case that is better understood in the literature (Tarlea and Freyberg-Inan 2018). It seeks to provide an understanding of the extent to which political parties in government have responded to different incentives when deciding on the reorganization of their education systems.

Two aspects of the ways in which governments have adapted HE provision to the labour market are considered comparatively: first, establishing relationships with specific employers, which has required significant investment on the part of the government; and, second, the introduction of quality assurance criteria in the financing mechanism of HE using public funding.

Even though political parties in government have rarely been considered in the literature or in public debate as active players in these reforms, they do play such a role and they have the opportunity to make use of their power when regulating HE (see also Busemeyer, Franzmann and Garritzmann 2013). While the role of the state has changed substantially since 1989 in CEE, somewhat ironically it continued to play an equally important role after the communist regimes collapsed.

However, political motivation cannot be regarded to be entirely separate from structural conditions in the economy, such as those determined by the labour market. I show that these political considerations – which are understood as the room to manoeuvre of political parties in government – are endogenous to the labour markets in these countries. Governments made efforts at coordination in order to build links between universities and the labour market. First, they introduced and financed study streams aimed at improving the goodness of fit of HE output to demands in the labour market; and, second, governments also introduced financing mechanisms intended to improve HE quality, switching the focus from input (e.g. number of students) to output (e.g. research productivity) indicators. The first aspect is more important in Hungary; the second has been more visible in Poland, thus far. This has led to different models of HE governance very much in line with different models of capitalism. An empirical analysis shows that, in response to the labour market, more forms of coordination have emerged in Hungary between employers and universities in comparison to Poland, which has evolved along a more liberal path.

1 Theoretical and empirical contribution

1.1 HE governance in a political-economic context

The theoretical framework developed here builds on political economy scholarship with a strong interest in skill formation, the varieties of capitalism (VoC) framework. HE governance understood as quality assurance and goodness of fit has not, to date, been explained in the VoC framework, in either new or old democracies. I show here, in a novel way, that it can help us explain HE dynamics in the post-communist world. One important tenet of this theoretical framework is that skill formation, understood as the processes through which individual countries create human capital – skills – is essential for the types of relationships that are established between the different political-economic institutions.

Hall and Soskice (2001) explained that modern democratic capitalist systems are not characterized by the same coordination mechanisms between the most important institutions in the economy. The authors distinguished between liberal and coordinated market economies. A liberal economy, such as the United States, is characterized by an education system that provides people with general skills. Coordinated market economies, such as Germany, provide individuals with more specific skills (Culpepper and Finegold 1999). In a liberal market economy, individuals obtain more specific training on-the-job, while in coordinated economies these highly specific skills for the industry in which employees are active are provided by a formal education system. Hall and Soskice (2001) explain that skills provided by education institutions, by either vocational training in coordinated economies or more general education in liberal economies, are complementary to the needs of the labour market. As a result, employers are also well adapted to this existing skill pool in the market. However, little is known about whether such coordination has emerged in the market economies of CEE with the exception of Hancké (2011), same with about what could explain the differences between Poland and Hungary.

I show here that similar, complementary institutions have emerged in CEE, but these have not been addressed in the literature either conceptually or empirically. I emphasize these institutions of skill formation by focusing on the critical role of the state in facilitating coordination between employers and HE institutions and by improving HE quality. I start the analysis with the work of Nölke and Vliegenthart (2009), which characterizes the countries of CEE as dependent market economies. This is a third variety of capitalism, joining the liberal and the coordinated market economies. Rationalizing the implications of this conceptualization, Tarlea (2015) explained how skill formation in CEE can be understood within this framework. The dependent market economy model is redefined in such a way as to allow skills to play a similarly central role as in the initial VoC formulation (Hall and Soskice 2001). The evolution of skill formation in CEE is explained in the context of the emergence of the dependent market economy in these countries. The labour markets for highly educated individuals have been fundamentally influenced by MNCs (Tarlea 2015).

Along similar lines, Tarlea and Freyberg-Inan (2018) characterized Romania as a low-skills equilibrium-dependent market economy. They explained that the low-skills equilibrium in goods and services in Romania is determined and sustained by the HE sector in the country, and showed that the most important employers in the market – MNCs – are key actors in supporting this low-skills equilibrium. Given the structure and types of activity developed in the region by MNCs, the relatively low quality of instruction and research in HE in Romania is complementary to the low-level requirements of firms that are active domestically. The demand for sophisticated labour is low in private and public firms, both domestic- and foreign-owned. However, the large, more productive firms tend to be MNCs (European Bank for Reconstruction and Development [EBRD] 2014). Given that MNCs do not need very sophisticated skills, students enrolled in university do not have incentives to invest in acquiring difficult-to-obtain skills. By having these two sets of actors following their interests, the outcome is what Tarlea and Freyberg-Inan (2018) call a low-skills equilibrium where relatively low-value-added activities are carried out by a relatively low-skilled labour force (Tarlea 2015).

The question addressed in this chapter is whether this relationship between employers, universities and governments can also explain the diverging policy changes in Poland and Hungary. Indeed, in this picture of overall low equilibrium, some companies active in some countries have managed to move up the ladder of economic sophistication; others, less so. This chapter engages with these theories and with their empirical implications and tests to what extent their scope conditions are more encompassing. The chapter therefore engages in a comparison of two relatively similar countries – Hungary and Poland – while treating Romania as a shadow case, better understood in the literature (Tarlea and Freyberg-Inan 2018).

The analysis relies importantly on the work of Dobbins (2011) on the Europeanization of HE in CEE. Key trends are emphasized in that research, such as the undeniable power of the Bologna process to change the organization of universities in the region. The Bologna reforms were a good opportunity for CEE countries to prove their commitment to the European project. Nevertheless, differences have emerged amongst the HE sectors despite the highly globalized network of European regulatory institutions pushing for a more homogenous European HE landscape. This divergence remains to be explained. The differences in how these relatively similar countries have changed their HE sectors can be explained by the internal dynamics of the labour market and by the active role of governments in HE reform. Indeed, Kwiek's insightful work on Poland showed how trends in HE has changed since the liberalization of the HE system was embraced and how the hard sciences started playing a more important role once governments recognized the importance of these areas of study in the labour market (Kwiek 2012).

1.2 Fit-for-purpose and HE quality

Widely accepted European criteria for measuring HE quality are not yet established (Leisyte and Westerheijden 2014). As Jones and Ratcliff (1999) pointed out, the proper goals and means of education are highly context- and stakeholder-dependent, while firms active in the labour market are key stakeholders. One aspect of HE quality is taken into account here – its fitness for purpose, which is closely linked, but not synonymous, with employability. It is a feature of HE that provides for a connection between employers and HE graduates. This link is especially vulnerable in instances in which market mechanisms have changed in fundamental ways.

Another indicator for HE quality captures the tension between enrolments and funding, and this aspect is taken into account in this chapter together with the introduction of quality criteria in funding mechanisms (Harvey and Green 1993; Harvey and Williams 2010). Also documented in other work (Kwiek 2012; Tarlea 2015), enrolment levels in HE have increased spectacularly in the two countries in the post-communist period. Nevertheless, spending patterns have not followed the same trend, and this has had a series of consequences for the ways in which funding was distributed locally, especially for study streams that are more expensive. Some governments have been particularly concerned about developments that influence this quality indicator, as both the Polish and Hungarian cases show.

Reforms aimed at improving the quality of HE and its fitness for purpose are more likely to be initiated and to succeed as long as political parties in power can benefit from the change, as developments in Polish reform, in the empirical part of the chapter, indicate. The Hungarian case shows how parties can politicize HE governance, as the Orbán government has done by directly targeting its constituency.[2] It implemented reforms aimed at restricting fresh HE graduates from working abroad. This found favour with voters having nationalistic views, unlike those who were cosmopolitan. The political factors driving changes in HE have changed both the design as well as the focus of studies.

This mechanism is likely to be perpetuated further. Political parties in power are also likely to benefit from the change if there is a demand in the market for higher skills, or if they can help create that demand, as some Hungarian governments did before 2010. The demand for higher skills comes from important employers in the market. Companies active domestically have changed as a consequence of market liberalization since the 1990s. A significantly important trend has been the entrance of MNCs into the market.

Certain measures by the government were important in attracting these foreign companies, one of them being the provision of human capital via the university system. Thus, MNCs active domestically have started to play a key role in the demand side for skills. They are important as desirable employers for fresh HE graduates and their presence is salient in these countries, which makes them important stakeholders in the HE sector (e.g. EBRD 2014).

2 A comparative perspective on Poland and Hungary

The functioning of markets in goods and services in virtually all areas has been dramatically reconfigured since the fall of communism (e.g. Stark and Bruszt 1998; Svejnar 1999). Interactions between key actors in given structures have determined different outcomes in reforms, including the governance of HE. This sector has seen the most spectacular evolution in the post-communist era, with very rapidly increasing levels of enrolment, from around 15 per cent to more than 60 per cent across the region (United Nations Educational, Scientific and Cultural Organization [UNESCO] 2016). However, the development of funding for HE has not been similarly spectacular. One factor that has allowed for these diverging trends has been a more flexible approach to HE quality, as this empirical part argues. Poland and Hungary have been successful in the post-communist period, both economically and politically. This has had direct consequences for the development of HE in both countries, especially in contrast to other countries of the region, such as Romania (Tarlea and Freyberg-Inan 2018). However, developments in HE have not followed a monotonic trend in Hungary and Poland.

The following case studies provide a narrative of the HE policies promoted by various political parties in different contexts in the two countries. I emphasize the types of incentives that parties seem to be responsive to when engaging in reforms in HE and how these reforms have a direct, measurable impact on HE governance. I focus in particular on the relationship to an important stakeholder group in HE quality: employers. I explain why these reforms have differed in the two countries and explain the complex mechanisms driving HE reform.

2.1 Hungary

2.1.1 The emergence of coordination between employers and universities

To put it in its historical context, the reform of Hungarian HE began before the 1980s. Lajos (1993: 404) emphasized the bilateral intergovernmental agreements, the support of the Soros Foundation, as well as the incentives and funding for university courses taught in different foreign languages. This was important for the internationalization of Hungarian universities in the 1980s, and it therefore preceded the political changes of the 1990s. At the same time, cooperation between universities and industry had already started at the end of the 1960s. Short-cycle professional HE has a long tradition in Hungary – for example, the schools of engineering and the agricultural academies (Lajos 1993: 404): Hungary has a dual HE system composed of colleges and universities. Moreover, in the period following 1990, HE enrolment has increased the most in the public sector.

The first democratically elected government, headed by Prime Minister Antall, was a right-wing government led by the Hungarian Democratic Forum. Funding was not as problematic in Hungary as in the rest of the Eastern European region, especially at the beginning of the 1990s, due to a "relatively favourable government policy" (Lajos 1993: 403). But, most significantly, secondary vocational schools continue to be important and more students are enrolled in vocational schools than in other secondary schools. As Hancké (2012) also emphasized, this distinguishes Hungary from Poland, Romania and Estonia, where vocational training has almost disappeared.

2.1.2 The evolution of coordination

Similarly, Hungarian governments have played an essential role in building links between HE institutions and MNCs, especially in the period 2000–2010. Successive governments have played an active role in building the educational infrastructure and in fostering links with MNCs. Probably the most important aspect of the measures undertaken by the Hungarian socialist governments of Medgyessy, Gyurcsány and Bajnai between 2002 and 2010 is that they provided first the infrastructure necessary for these businesses, including the development of HE. Moreover, successive governments have actively pursued a policy of attracting foreign direct investment to this sector. Strategies for this have included state aid and subsequently lower corporate taxes and investment in HE. The automotive sector has become Hungary's comparative global strength, also emphasized by PricewaterhouseCoopers's studies (PwC 2014). The government provided the infrastructure necessary for businesses active locally by ensuring the supply of much-needed local skilled labour (Economist Intelligent Unit 2012). This was achieved by relying on the educational infrastructure in HE. I show, as follows, that when Audi entered the Hungarian market it required HE graduates in engineering; the government eased the process by supplying the skills that were required. It also provided Volkswagen with financial incentives (direct subsidies and low taxation) for the relocation of the company and, subsequently, to elevate the level of sophistication of the activities it carries out in Hungary. This cooperation between the government and different producers in the automotive sector showcase the mechanisms for the creation of links between employers and HE institutions. However, and emphatically, this does not exclude the possibility that cooperation can occur in other sectors as well. Equally, it is not always easy to create the link between employers, universities and young graduates.

Cooperation also occurred in the case of Audi. In 1993 the Hungarian government, headed by prime-minister Antall, was successful in attracting investment from Audi, a company of the Volkswagen group, to Győr in western Hungary. Between 1993 and 2014 Audi invested a total of €5.7 billion (Tury 2014). A policy of maintaining Audi's interest in Hungary was pursued further by the government through action taken to develop a high-skilled base of graduates tailored to meet the requirements of this MNC. As early as 2007 the Audi Hungary Vehicle Engineering Department Group was launched, as a part of the Department of Applied Mechanics at the Széchenyi István University of Győr. The university offers higher apprenticeships, similar to the German system, as well as bachelor's degrees, master's degrees and PhD-level training. Unsurprisingly, the department's website is fully available in German and Hungarian, although not in English. The faculty is expected to train future employees for the manufacturer in Győr. The government's role in this process is emphasized further, particularly since Audi does not appear to have provided financial support to the university. The government justified this incentive package by reference to the beneficial relationship that would be developed with the University of Győr (Tury 2014 provides good descriptive evidence of this). This points yet again to the fact that Hungary evolved more clearly into a coordinated dependent market economy and that HE provision is supportive of this.

Indeed, in 2014, Volkswagen manufactured in Győr what PwC (2014) would call "advanced automotive for Audi. In this branch Audi manufactures engines, assembles vehicles and carries out technical developments closely linked to the production cycle. Engineers are expected to understand advanced processes and to be able to supervise automated production. The branch in Hungary therefore requires some highly skilled HE graduates: "complete engine development exists only in Germany, and in Hungary only partial tasks are being carried out" (Tury 2014).

This is typical for a dependent market economy. While the main part of development is still being carried out at Ingolstadt, Neckarsulm and Wolfsburg in Germany, the level of technological cooperation between branches ensures that there is substantial scope for the Hungarian automotive industry to cooperate with the universities in Hungary. A closer analysis of the investment made in business promotion shows that the Hungarian government commissioned PwC, a management consultancy, to assist with the government's efforts to attract investment: PwC has branches in Budapest and Győr. The investment agency advertises the education level of its employees as the biggest asset of the economy: "the Hungarian automotive sector's cooperation with the local education system is strong and focuses on research and development" (PwC, 2014). This shows the strong incentives Audi had in supporting the university sector in building links to the companies active locally. However, the relationship between businesses and universities is not necessarily one without troubles, as later developments proved.

These reforms built on the work of previous governments. In spring 2008 the government headed by Ferenc Gyurcsány of the Hungarian Socialist Party (Magyar Szocialista Párt [MSZP]) had already attempted to introduce moderate (€550) fees to be paid yearly by all students as part of its deficit-cutting reform package. However, a nationwide referendum in March 2008 rejected the package and the introduction of tuition fees was banned. Thus, a left-oriented government decided not to make HE budget cuts: the government was responsive to voters' concerns regarding HE. Orbán could still benefit from the decisions that were made while the previous government was in power. This is a telling example of what Pierson (2004) refers to as the time lag between decisions being made and their effects on institutions. In fact, Daimler Mercedes started manufacturing cars in Kecskemet in 2012: the decision to build the factory was made in June 2008 while Ferenc Gyurcsány of the Hungarian Socialist Party – MSZP – was in power. Daimler responded to state efforts to develop vocational training in the Kecskemet region, according to the existing cooperation agreement with the government. As was noted in the magazine Business Week, "Hungary's allure is an educated labor force that last year cost €8.61 an hour compared with €45.66 in Germany, according to the German auto industry group" (*Business Week* 2012). This highlights Orbán's ambivalent relationship with investors. He argues that he is supportive of large industrial investments, particularly in the manufacturing sector, but he has declared repeatedly his lack of trust in foreign investors, especially those in banking or the media; he has even acted on this by introducing a set of new taxes on these businesses, as reported by Reuters: "companies hit by the taxes include Hungarian units of Deutsche Telekom and EON, and the main local lobby group for German firms say they feel separating investors into good and bad groups is counterproductive" (Dunai 2012). This different attitude of the Orbán government to investors also shows that the government does not necessarily need to be a continuous supporter of strong links with the business environment. As a result, the relationship between employers and universities can be particularly vulnerable in its incipient stage. The analyses on Poland also seem to identify some inconsistencies amongst policymakers regarding HE.

2.1.3 Quality assurance mechanisms in Hungary

Hungarian HE received significant attention from close observers of European politics when, in 2010, the Orbán government started a controversial process of HE reforms, including massive budget cuts. This is an example of a non-incremental HE development, showing that the active decisions of governments influence HE spending. In this instance the government had stated that, in the longer term, HE should be "self-financing" (Fuzessi 2013). Orbán's cabinet was invested in May 2010, following the formation of a super majority coalition headed by the right-wing Hungarian Civic Union (Magyar Polg ri Sz vets g – Fidesz) and the Christian Democratic People's Party (KDNP). In 2011 the government reduced the number of scholarships drastically, which led to a 25 per cent drop in the number of HE applicants in 2012 (Fuzessi 2013). Students on government scholarships were required to sign a contract in which they promised that they would work in Hungary for a period, within the next 20 years, of twice the length of their course (Fuzessi 2013). While this was a response of the far right to the challenges of integration in the European common market and an attempt to keep its highly educated skill pool in the country, it also provides some indication that HE can be used quite efficiently by parties to target their own constituencies. The government appealed more to nationalistic ideals and less so to the structure or the needs of the economy, such as the necessity to attract highly skilled labour at home. One reason why this has been a notoriously contested reform is the fact that the government has not incentivized the different institutional actors, choosing instead to force students to stay in the country through formal requirements.

Universities in Hungary are relatively autonomous. The Hungarian Accreditation Committee carries out the evaluations for quality assurance in HE, but the share of funding distributed according to quality criteria is low. In 2008 universities received around 15 per cent of their funding from third-party funding, 70 per cent came from the state and 15 per cent from tuition fees (Vasilache, Temesi and Dima 2012). For Poland, the respective data were 34 per cent from business, 59 per cent from government and 7 per cent from abroad (Eurostat 2010). Similarly, most research grants from the Hungarian education ministry stemmed from operational grants rather than competitive grants. (Vasilache, Temesi and Dima 2012). This shows little commitment to HE quality provision, even in a regional perspective.

2.2 The rise of far-right parties and higher education in Hungary and Poland

The rise of populism in Europe after the global financial crisis that started in 2007 and that has continued to have repercussions well into 2018 has been well documented (e.g. Mudde 2017). Increasing populism has been documented across Europe, but Hungary is a frontrunner in this respect, followed closely by Poland. Populism has been coupled with scepticism towards the European Union, also in old European Union member states, such as the UK, France or the Netherlands (De Vries 2018). The rise of illiberalism or of the so-called Hungarian goulash democracy that seems to entail both populism and Euroscepticism has caught the attention of scholars and the media and is considered a real threat to the country's democracy (Grzymala-Busse 2017; *The Economist* 2018). Furthermore, mirroring developments have taken place in Poland as well. In the words of Anna Grzymala-Busse (2017: 4), "In Poland and Hungary, populist parties are governing and dismantling the formal institutions of liberal democracy".

In Hungary, Viktor Orbán secured a third mandate in April 2018, when his Fidesz party won a two-thirds majority in parliament (*The Economist* 2018). Jobbik, the nationalist party, that has been moving to the centre, came second. Orbán's campaign was directed against migrants and international, including European, threats. At the same time, populists lost some electoral support in between 2011 and 2013 in Poland (Grzymala-Busse 2017: 5). But, while many aspects of governing the economy and the polity are influenced by this increase in populism, we refrain to referring to developments in the field of HE. We do this with two purposes: first, to show that HE governance in the two countries is responsive to domestic political concerns, and particularly to the concerns of parties in power; and second, to emphasize how well-connected the education sector is to other institutions in the political economy.

The ruling parties in the two countries have taken over the Constitutional Courts and issued new laws that constrain liberal norms (Grzymala-Busse 2017: 6). Similar developments to those in Hungary have also taken place in Poland. After obtaining an absolute majority in the 2015 election, the Law and Justice Party (PiS) "began first with a controversy over the Constitutional Court: the new government refused to seat judges nominated by the previous, and instead insisted both on naming the replacements and curtailing the power of the Court. PiS then attacked the media, with directors of the public TV and radio stations and critical journalists being fired and replaced" (Grzymala-Busse 2017: 7).

Viktor Orbán's policy against HE in Hungary has been rather visible. In March 2017, new HE legislation was passed that would in effect force the Central European University (CEU) in Budapest to shut down (British Broadcasting Corporation 2017). The law stipulated that an agreement was necessary between the home government of the university and the Hungarian in order for HE institutions to function there. The effect was that CEU would not be able to function in Hungary (Matthews 2017). In the same vein, the humanities and social sciences have suffered most since Orbán came to power in 2010. Liviu Mateiu, the provost of the CEU argues that Orbán tends to perceive HE as a "luxury" good and that Hungary would need fewer students, not more in Orbán's view. Hungary's characteristics as a dependent market economy seems to have hit home with Orbán. CEU, Norbert Sabic of CEU, argues that "Orbán has turned his back on the 'knowledge economy' orthodoxy – of which mass HE is a key part – after witnessing Hungary's failure to catch up with Western European economies following the fall of communism" (Matthews 2017). Orbán's vision seems to be that Hungary should become interested in becoming a cheap manufacturing hub for German companies. Such a debate comes to show very clearly how the structure of the economy and the electoral consequences that derive therein are not ignored by savvy politicians.

Indeed, Hungary has cut down spending on HE in the wake of the financial crisis more so than other countries in Europe or worldwide. The compulsory school leaving years have been cut from 18 to 16 in 2011. This means that the number of students eligible to go to university has gone down by more than 30 per cent (Matthews 2017). To further emphasize that education is paid from public money, students receive letters from the government in which they are informed how much the state has paid for their education (BBC 2017).

All this comes to show that skill formation and HE, particularly, are under clear supervision of the government. Even more so, education policy has been used rather effectively by the Orbán government against voters who are not his constituency. Moreover, his policies seem to cater effectively to his constituency, which has no interest in HE but rather in preserving and enhancing their own status.

2.3 Poland

2.3.1 The emergence of coordination between employers and universities

While the reform of HE in Hungary has taken centre stage in the region and has led to street protests, Poland has also witnessed significant changes in HE. However, the HE systems in the two countries have evolved along surprisingly different paths.

The HE sector has traditionally been structured differently in Poland compared to Hungary. Polish communist HE did not benefit from an institutional framework that would allow for cooperation between universities and firms active domestically. Moreover, both the more liberal development of HE and the more distant connection to the labour market have been maintained in the post-communist era. A skill formation system developed in the country more closely resembling a liberal education system than one providing specific skills typical for a coordinated system. A natural consequence of having a different skill formation system in place in the beginning of transition has been that subsequent decisions to reform HE had different sources (understood as stakeholders) than in Hungary. The governments in power had a more direct influence on HE governance; this was not linked directly to employers, and improving HE quality was more direct. Also, the relationship of universities to employers is less straightforward, but there is scope for cooperation. A different type of cooperation between the state and private firms active domestically has been at play in Poland historically, with universities providing general skills tailored less to the specific requirements of employers. The post-communist governments, starting with that elected in 1993, have not reversed this communist legacy.

2.3.2 The evolution of weak coordination

Important changes were implemented under HE minister Barbara Kudrycka, who was in office between 2007 and 2013. Moreover, discussions regarding a reform of HE continue to be on the public agenda following the 2015 parliamentary elections. A member of the Civic Platform, Kudrycka introduced controversial but progressive HE reforms – a cut in enrolment, especially in certain fields. She was a member of the Tusk government, an example of an economically liberal government preparing reforms in HE likely to be supportive of the domestic economy and, most importantly, having an impact on the quality of education provision. The changes in government in this case have also had effects on the spending and enrolment ratio in the country (Tarlea 2015). Kudrycka introduced a law designed to prevent this over-commitment of university professors by binding them to full-time employment in one university. Similar to Romania, a ranking of universities was introduced in Poland, according to which research funds would be distributed. These reforms resulted in a reshuffling of the entire HE system. Above all, however, the reform had significant implications for the quality of the education provided: one direct implication was higher spending per student. However, because parliamentary elections were approaching, Kudrycka resigned at the end of 2013 as a result of her too controversial reforms. Minister Kolarska-Bobińska took over the education portfolio after Prime Minister Donald Tusk's reshuffle in November 2013.

The Civic Platform government understood the need to incentivize students to invest in skills rather than coerce them not to leave the country. This distinguishes it from the Orbán government in Hungary. Reforms aimed at improving the quality of HE are more likely to be initiated and to succeed as long as the political parties in power can benefit from the change. The Civic Platform, which benefitted from the support of the somewhat urban middle class, was more likely to take the risk of implementing these controversial reforms. The controversial reform introduced by Barbara Kudrycka aimed to improve the entire HE sector and to reshuffle the equilibrium between the losers and the winners of these reforms. Even more significant, what is specific to this more liberal variety of capitalism in the dependent market economy of Poland is its top-down approach, started by the government and with no particular cooperation of employers as important stakeholders in the process. Kudrycka was particularly active in this pursuit.

Nevertheless, other similarities between Poland and Hungary have become more noticeable since the 2015 elections in Poland. In addition, far-right policies have also taken centre-stage in the country. An analogous debate to that in Hungary is also taking place in Poland regarding the right to free education. In 2016, discussions have been held regarding the appropriateness of free education for medical students: the cost of educating one medical student, by the end of their six-year studies, amounts to around €66,000 euros (11,000 per year). Maciej Hamankiewicz from Poland's Medical Council complained that graduates in medicine find foreign countries more attractive, while Poland is experiencing an increasing shortage of medical staff (Polish News Agency 2016).

It is a fact that the Law and Justice Party (PiS) and its leader Jarosław Kaczyński are generally suspicious of foreign influence (Foy 2016). The discussion the need of universities to attract students, i.e. to be entrepreneurial is also salient in Poland. Kaczyński believes there is a need for new education policies (Foy 2016). Unlike its predecessor, the Law and Justice Party represents those that have benefitted less from the transition to a market economy. These are the people at the bottom of the income distribution, and the PiS government seems to be responding to these concerns as well. This shows some similarities to what takes place in Hungary.

All in all, instances of cooperation between the government and private firms in Poland are less numerous, and such developments have not been as central as in Hungary. Examples of this do exist in Poland, such as the cooperation of the technology company Google with a business school in Warsaw that started in 2015 and which was intended to foster entrepreneurship in the region (Stanislawska 2015). However, the government was less involved in this project, which has developed more organically, as a cooperative venture between a private university and a private firm. It should come as no surprise to find more instances of cooperation of local branches of MNCs with education providers in Poland, either. Indeed, the consulting firm Deloitte (2014) provides a more comprehensive overview of the different programs developed at national level in Poland aimed at improving the cooperation of private firms with universities. These programs provide a legislative framework that should allow for this cooperation, rather than the government becoming closely involved in specific relationships between universities and private employers.

This emphasizes the more liberal orientation of the country in comparison to Hungary. It also underlines once more that there is more than one way to achieve success in a democratic market economy, which is very much in line with the tradition of VoC. Interestingly, cooperation between universities and businesses is also possible in this framework; it can happen without the government being particularly active in pursuing cooperation. Nevertheless, unlike in Hungary, this close collaboration of businesses and universities is less likely if incentives for cooperation are not present, if firms and education providers do not believe they are benefitting from direct collaboration. The case study on Hungary showed that the government was able to intervene to create incentives for cooperation.

2.3.3 Quality assurance in Poland

From a broader perspective, and similar to the rest of the region, Polish HE has expanded, a consequence of the liberalization of the market for education. However, some fields have expanded more than others. Kwiek (2012) showed how the expansion era in Polish HE lasted for about 15 years, from 1990 to 2005, and that this upward trend in enrolment has slowly started to change. Most interestingly, the model of the Polish HE system has allowed for the burgeoning of private universities. This development was in contrast to the situation in Hungary but similar to that in other countries in the region, such as the Baltic countries, Romania or Bulgaria. One consequence of this market mechanism in HE has been the fact that universities in both the private and the public sectors have become particularly interested in attracting a large number of students (Grove 2014); this enabled them to secure funding. A larger proportion of students is enrolled in private HE institutions than in

Hungary. While Kaczyński's Law and Justice Party was in power, before 2007, HE governance simply developed in a laissez-faire fashion.

Kwiek argues that, as a consequence, Polish universities have, paradoxically, become even more teaching oriented than they once were. During communism, HE instruction was separated from research and the purpose of the university was to provide instruction. Therefore, the argument that universities have become even more teaching-oriented is a strong criticism of HE developments, especially for the quality of education provided in these institutions. The fields that have experienced the greatest expansion are also those that have done poorly, especially when their research output is analyzed. We are dealing with a university system divided between soft and hard fields, similar to the situations in Estonia and Romania (Tomusk 2000).

Performance-based funding for research is relatively new in Europe: the very first such programs to be introduced were in Belgium in 1985 (Organisation for Economic Cooperation and Development [OECD] 2010: 90, 2016; European Commission 2010). Furthermore, in 2010 no single country used a 100 per cent performance-based system of funding. So, it should come as no surprise that performance-based funding is also new in post-communist Europe.

We observed some differences between Poland and Hungary: Poland uses purpose-specific funding while Hungary relies on an input-based mechanism. This means that in Hungary 91 per cent of funding is based on inputs, such as the number of students enrolled (Eurydice 2011). In Poland, 70 per cent of the total public contributions to HE are provided for specific purposes, directly linked to functions, tasks and objectives (Eurydice 2011: 38). In contrast to Hungary, Poland was already using output criteria in the 1990s.

The introduction of a performance-based indicator was not without problems in Poland. An important reform took place in 2008 with the aim of improving innovativeness (Polish Ministry for Science and Higher Education 2009). This was amended by the law passed on March 18, 2011 (Eurydice 2011: 86). A side effect was that it favoured competition, rather than cooperation, between universities. The government is continuing its work on the performance assessment system that is meant to foster collaboration between national innovation systems and universities. However, this collaboration continues to be less substantial than in Hungary.

Conclusions

This analysis of the political and economic nature of HE reforms shows that the regulation of HE in Hungary and in Poland has been a matter of contention between political parties. Parties catering to different constituencies have pursued different policies once in government. This happened in both countries when parties targeting the middle classes pursued different reforms to those catering to lower-income individuals and families. These reforms have been relevant in political debates and have even led to street protests. Most importantly, however, change has not always been in the same direction. This nonlinearity is expected to continue in the years to come. Equally importantly, these reforms in HE have built on existing traditions understood as historical legacies in the education sector and in the relationship of firms with universities. Governments can build on pre-existing conditions, such as the inherited industrial structure together with the inherited university structure. This interplay between political parties, universities and firms, each pursuing their interests, has determined the different HE reforms in the two countries. This relationship explains the puzzle identified at the beginning of this chapter, the different HE regimes in two otherwise relatively similar countries.

The analysis shows that governments can strongly influence HE governance in a variety of ways: political parties influenced HE governance by targeting the fitness for purpose of HE – that is, its relationship to employers, as well as quality criteria in HE funding. The most important channel in Hungary has been the attempt to build relationships with MNCs in order to attract these to the country and to keep them active locally by providing the necessary human capital. This has simultaneously fostered the demand and the supply of technical skills, which have had an important positive effect on the development of HE quality in the country. It has allowed education to develop more closely alongside the labour market and thus to make HE fit for purpose. Other actions have also proved effective, such as the attempts of Polish governments to incentivize students and university staff to invest in skills, by providing funding through either tuition or better pay and a reduction of the workload of academic staff, which were important quality criteria. Even in contexts where the relationship of HE provision to the demand for skills in the labour market has been less direct, the existence of a qualified skill pool was essential in attracting business to the country, as the case of Google in Poland emphasizes.

Developments in Hungary show that the country is highly dependent on MNCs, which makes it a good and clear example of a dependent market economy. At the same time, there is strong cooperation between institutions of skill formation and universities and providers of vocational training, which shows strong characteristics of coordination. Most importantly, however, it shows that, sooner or later, skills develop very much in line with the "spirit" of coordination typical of the country. Poland is also highly dependent on MNCs, but the links between universities and companies arise in a different way. Governments incentivize students, rather than companies, to invest in skills.

Poland is a more liberal dependent market economy, and the skills provided by universities tend to be more general, which resembles the HE system in the UK. But, most importantly, both coordination mechanisms – liberal and coordinated – can be effective in fostering skill formation in the economy. Both have their specific weaknesses, which need to be tackled with policies; and the most obvious promoter of these policies identified in this chapter has been the government. Political parties in government can have a clear vision about the needs of the labour market and they can incentivize companies, students and even university staff to invest in education and, thus, to promote quality in HE. However, the political parties seem to use this understanding in order to please their voters. The extent to which parties cater to their constituencies is systematic, and whether it falls along partisan lines, such as the left–right spectrum, should be analyzed in future research. Nevertheless, what can be claimed with certainty is that the support of parties in government can lead developments into one direction or another. This can become an important hurdle for HE development in the region.

Somehow ironically, the state, as represented by the political parties in government, has rediscovered its role in the economy, and this role can be used fruitfully. A radically different vision of the government can have dramatic consequences for HE and for the political economy more generally. This is the reason why this chapter emphasizes that it is not entirely clear that Hungary will continue on its path of coordinating businesses with education provision; nor is it entirely certain that Poland will continue on its neoliberal path.

However, change is expected to occur – albeit with difficulty. While much of the public discussion on education reform has focused on the inability of governments or on the restrictions imposed by the scarcity of public finances, or by the clear and strict guidelines of European reforms, this chapter highlights how governments can and do play an important role even in such less friendly environments. One fact is here to stay: it would be extremely difficult to analyze the quality of HE when separated from labour market dynamics and their political determinants. Other factors influence HE governance, amongst which are the Europeanization and the globalization processes of which all CEE countries are a part. The level of professionalism of HE officials will also play a role. Just how important these roles are should be considered in future research.

Notes

1 This chapter is an adapted and updated version of an article by Tarlea (2017). Higher education governance in Central and Eastern Europe: A perspective on Hungary and Poland. *European Educational Research Journal, 16*(5): 670–683.

2 Viktor Orbán has been Prime Minister of Hungary, for the second time, since 2010. See www.kormany.hu/en/the-prime-minister/the-prime-minister (accessed 18 October 2016).

References

Bohle, D. and Greskovits, B. (2012) *Capitalist diversity on Europe's periphery.* Ithaca, NY: Cornell University Press.

British Broadcasting Corporation (2017) "Hungary passes bill that targets Central European University", April 4. Available at: www.bbc.com/news/world-europe-39493758 (Accessed: 30 June 2018).

Busemeyer, M.R. and Trampusch, C. (2011) "Review article: Comparative political science and the study of education", *British Journal of Political Science*, 41(2): 413–443.

Busemeyer, M.R., Franzmann, S.T., and Garritzmann, J.L. (2013) "Who owns education? Cleavage structures in the partisan competition over educational expansion", *West European Politics*, 36(3): 521–546.

Business Week (2012) "Daimler's billion dollar bet on Hungary", www.bloomberg.com/news/articles/2012-04-05/daimlers-billion-dollar-bet-on-hungary (Accessed 13 September 2018).

Culpepper, P.D. and Finegold, D. (1999) *The German skills machine: Sustaining comparative advantage in a global economy.* Oxford: Berghahn Books.

De Vries, C.E. (2018) *Euroscepticism and the future of European integration.* Oxford: Oxford University Press.

Deloitte (2014) *Country profile: Poland – Researcher's report.* Available at: http://ec.europa.eu/euraxess/pdf/research_policies/country_files/Poland_Country_Profile_RR 2014_FINAL.pdf (Accessed: 28 February 2016).

Dobbins, M. (2011) *Higher education policies in Central and Eastern Europe: Convergence towards a common model?*Basingstoke: Palgrave MacMillan.

Dunai, M. (2012) "New Daimler company may help Hungary avoid recession", *Reuters.* Available at: www.reuters.com/article/us-hungary-daimler-idUSBRE82F192201 20316 (Accessed: 14 November 2016).

The Economist (2018) "Hungary's illiberal prime minister Hungary's illiberal prime minister, wins a landslide: Fears for the country's democracy deepen. Available at: www.economist.com/europe/2018/04/09/hungarys-illiberal-prime-minister-viktor-orb an-wins-a-landslide (Accessed: 10 June 2018).

Economist Intelligence Unit (2012) *Automotive report: Hungary.* London: Economist Intelligence Unit. Available at: www.eiu.com (Accessed: 19 October 2016).

European Bank for Reconstruction and Development (EBRD) (2014) *Annual indicators.* Available at: www.ebrd.com/what-we-do/economic-research-and-data/data/fore casts-macro-data-transitionindicators.html (Accessed: 14 November 2016).

European Commission (2010) "Efficiency and effectiveness of public expenditure on tertiary education in the EU", European Economy Occasional Papers, 70. Brussels: EC (DG Economic and Financial Affairs).

Eurostat (2010) *Foreign affiliated statistics.* Brussels: European Commission.

Eurydice (2011) *Modernisation of higher Education in Europe: Funding and the social dimension.* Available at: http://eacea.ec.europa.eu/education/eurydice/documents/thematic_reports/131en.pdf (Accessed: 10 August 2016).

Foy, H. (2016) "Jaroslaw Kaczynski: Poland's kingmaker", *Financial Times*, February 26.

Fuzessi, K. (2013) *Higher education under threat in Hungary.* Available at: www.opendemocracy.net/can-europe-make-it/k%C3%A1roly-f%C3%BCzessi/higher-education -under-threat-in-hungary (Accessed: 14 November 2016).

Grove, J. (2014) "Shrinking enrolments in Poland", *Times Higher Education*, March 6. Available at: www.insidehighered.com/news/2014/03/06/universities-poland-struggle-shrinking-enrollments (Accessed: 28 February 2016).

Grzymala-Busse, A. (2017) "Global populisms and their impact", *Slavic Review*, 76 (S1): S3–S8.

Hall, P. and Soskice, D. (eds). (2001) *Varieties of capitalism: The institutional foundations of competitiveness.* Oxford: Oxford University Press.

Hancké, B. (2011) Endogenous coordination: multinational companies and the production of collective goods in central and eastern Europe. LSE "Europe in Question", Discussion Paper Series, LEQS Paper No. 41/2011. Available at: www.lse.ac.uk/europeanInstitute/LEQS%20Discussion%20Paper%20Series/LEQSPaper41.pdf (Accessed: 19 October 2016).

Hancké, B. (2012) *Multinational companies and the production of collective goods in Central and Eastern Europe*. Cheltenham: Edward Elgar Publishing: 295–308.

Harvey, L. and Green, D. (1993) "Defining quality: Assessment and evaluation", *Higher Education*, 18(1): 9–34.

Harvey, L. and Williams, J. (2010) "Fifteen years of *Quality in Higher Education*", *Quality in Higher Education*, 16(1): 3–36.

Jones, E.A. and Ratcliff, J.L. (1999) "Global perspectives on program assessment and accreditation" in Strydom, A.H., Lategan, L., Muller, L., and Stetar, J. (eds), *Programme Assessment in Higher Education in South Africa*. Blomfontein, RSA: Unit for Higher Education Research, University of the Orange Free State.

Kwiek, M. (2012) "Changing higher education policies: From the deinstitutionalization to the re-institutionalization of the research mission in Polish universities", *Science and Public Policy*, 39(5): 641–654.

Lajos, T. (1993) "Perspectives, hopes and disappointments: Higher education reform in Hungary", *European Journal of Education*, 28(4): 403–411.

Leisyte, L. and Westerheijden, D.F. (2014) "Stakeholders and quality assurance in higher education", in Eggins, H. (ed.), *Drivers and Barriers to Achieving Quality in Higher Education*: 83–97. Rotterdam: Sense Publishers.

Matthews, D. (2017) "The state of higher education in Hungary", *Times Higher Education*. Available at: www.timeshighereducation.com/features/the-state-of-higher-education-in-hungary (Accessed: 30 June 2018).

Mudde, C. (2017) 'Populism isn't dead. Here are five things you need to know about it'. Available at: www.theguardian.com/commentisfree/2017/jul/07/populism-dead-european-victories-centrists (Accessed: 25 June 2018).

Nölke, A. and Vliegenthart, A. (2009) "Enlarging the varieties of vapitalism: The emergence of dependent market economies in East Central Europe", *World Politics*, 61(4): 670–702.

Organisation for Economic Cooperation and Development (2010) *Performance-based funding for public research in tertiary education institutions: Workshop proceedings*. Paris: OECD Publishing.

Organisation for Economic Cooperation and Development (2016) "Performance-based funding for public research in tertiary education institutions", Web annex to *Performance-based funding for public research in tertiary education institutions: Workshop proceedings*. Available at: www.oecd.org/sti/sci-tech/46756874.pdf (Accessed: 15 August 2016).

Pierson, P. (2004) *Politics in time: History, institutions and social analysis*. Princeton, NJ: Princeton University Press.

Polish Ministry of Science and Higher Education (2009) 'The Polish research and funding landscape'. Available at: www.aspera-eu.org/images/stories/national_days/polish/4_stolarczyk.pdf (Accessed: 10 August 2016).

Polish News Agency (2016) 'Should Polish students pay for education?' Available at: www.thenews.pl/1/9/Artykul/237922,Should-Polish-medical-students-pay-for-education (Accessed: 14 November 2016).

PricewaterhouseCoopers (PwC) (2014) *PwC CEO Survey.* Bucharest: Pricewaterhouse Coopers Romania.

Stanislawska, A. (2015) "Spearheaded by experts at Google, Warsaw has created a hub for start-ups'. Available at: www.polska.pl/en/business-science/investments-projects/google-opens-campus-warsaw-techhub/ (Accessed: 28 February 2016).

Stark, D. and Bruszt, L. (1998) *Post-socialist pathways: Transforming politics and property in East Central Europe.* Cambridge: Cambridge University Press.

Svejnar, J. (1999) "Labor markets in the transitional Central and East European economies", in Ashenfelter, O. and Card, D. (eds), *Handbook of Labor Economics*, 3 (B): 2809–2857. Available at: http://econpapers.repec.org/bookchap/eeelabchp/3-42.htm (Accessed: 19 October 2016).

Tarlea, S. (2015) *Dependency and development in Central and Eastern Europe's new capitalist systems.* DPhil Thesis, University of Oxford, UK.

Tarlea, S. and Freyberg-Inan, A. (2018) "The education skills trap in a dependent market economy: Romania's case in the 2000s", *Communist and Post-Communist Studies*, 51(1): 49–61.

Tomusk, V. (2000) "When East meets West: Decontextualizing the quality of East European higher education", *Quality in Higher Education*, 6(3): 175–185.

Tury, G. (2014) *Study on Latin America, the Caribbean and Central and Eastern Europe: Potential for economic exchange.* Hamburg: EU-LAC Foundation. Available at: https://eulacfoundation.org/en/system/files/EULAC%20Foundation%20Study%20LAC_CEECS_EN.pdf (Accessed: 14 November 2016).

UNESCO (2016) *UNESCO Data on Education.* Paris: UNESCO Institute for Statistics.

Vasilache, S., Temesi, J., and Dima, A. (2012) "Higher education reforms in Eastern Europe: A Hungarian–Romanian case study", *Management and Marketing*, 7(2): 295–322.

4 Low- and high-skills equilibria

What role for the government?

Introduction

The previous chapters have shown how a multitude of factors can determine the incentives of governments and businesses to invest in skills. In this chapter, we focus on how parties in government can influence the sophistication of the economy and on their motivations when doing so. A policy analysis in Poland and Romania between 1989 and 2015 shows how governments can determine a change in the supply of skills even in these relatively new democracies. We tackle the variation in the supply of sophisticated skills in the two countries and find that, unlike governments dominated by national-conservative parties, governments dominated by liberal parties have strategically steered the supply of skills in the economy. They have simultaneously identified and incentivized three key actors to invest in higher added value activities. They have steered their higher education (HE) institutions towards (i) offering degrees conducive to research and development (R&D), (ii) they have incentivized students through scholarships or through secure employment by fostering links with enterprises (iii) and they have bargained with multinational companies (MNCs) to attract sophisticated activities.

Political economists have long argued that political parties have more than a marginal role in economic policy-making (Hall 1986; Rodrik 1996), but this is far from agreed upon in the context of post-communist Central and Eastern Europe (CEE) (Bohle and Greskovits 2007, 2012). Whether political parties in government influence these new political economies other than by liberalizing the market is still unsettled in the literature (Bruszt and Greskovits 2009; Roberts 2009; Tarlea 2015).

Partisan differences in the field of HE in which political parties have been shown to have an impact in advanced industrial economies (Busemeyer 2015). Other scholars have similarly argued that government strategies directly influence the skills supply in the economy (Boix 1997; Jenssen 2011). Formally, the skills supply is measured through formal qualifications in the market, such as the number or the percentage of people who graduate from a specific degree each year.[1] This measure allows us to engage with the puzzling developments that have taken place in CEE between 1989 and 2015. While all countries have democratized and opened up their economies to international trade and investment, only some have moved from low- to high-skills equilibria in the production of goods and services. Equally, the skills supply through universities has also differed rather starkly both within and across countries.

Poland and Romania have simultaneously embarked on their paths towards democracy and a market economy. Notwithstanding, the research intensity of their economies has diverged, which is captured by the different trends in private and public R&D spending in both countries.[2] Other indicators regarding research intensity of these economies show a similar pattern. The number of researchers working in R&D[3] was 1,300 per million people in both countries in 1996. These numbers gradually diverged: they decreased in Romania while increasing in Poland. As such, in 2014 the number of researchers being active in R&D was 2,000 per million people in Poland and 900 in Romania. While these diverging trends capture the R&D intensity of entire economies, similarly diverging trends can be observed regarding general HE spending by the government. In 2012, Romania spent 0.8 per cent of GDP per capita on HE, the same as in 2001. Poland spent 1.1 per cent of GDP in 2012, up from 0.8 per cent in 2001 (UNESCO 2017).

One intriguing question emerges: what processes led to this divergence in economic sophistication? We trace the process that links the supply of skills to the economic sophistication of an economy and enquire what role

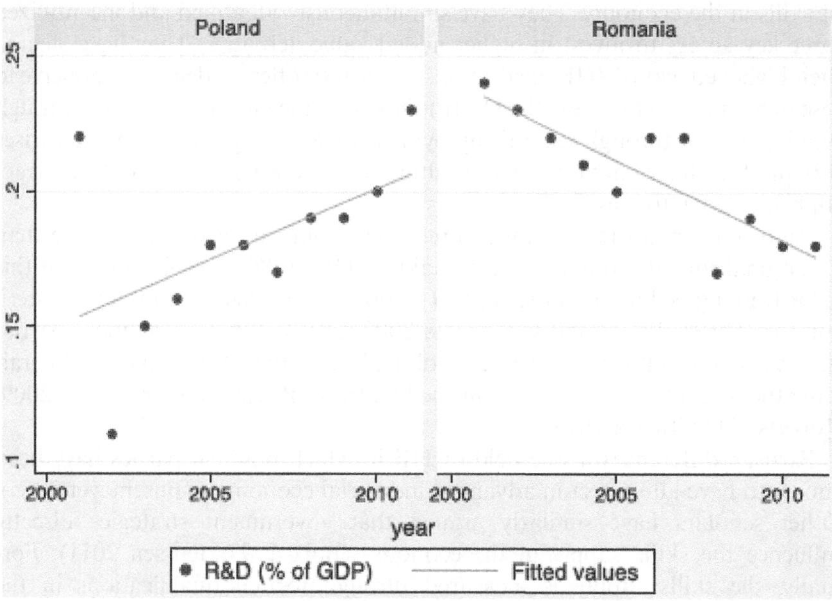

Figure 4.1 Research and development (R&D) as percentage of GDP in Romania and Poland

Source: Eurostat.

governments and political parties therein have played in the process. Education and training are a *sine qua non* condition in order for people to be able to engage in R&D intensive activities. Moreover, expenditure for R&D activities are in part financed by governments. Increasing the supply of sophisticated skills is one way through which the government can contribute towards more R&D-intensive activities taking place domestically, which is unquestionably a concern for policy-makers around the world (WEF 2012).

But the sophistication level of economic activities results from the interaction of a series of factors. For exploring this, we first consider the stakeholders that can influence the upgrading of skills supply and of the sophistication of domestic economic activities. We show why firms active domestically are less likely to be the leading actors in the upgrading process.[4] We move on to explain how other actors, such as chambers of commerce and HE institutions, can pursue higher value-added activities, but they tend not to get involved in such activities in the dependent market economies (DMEs) of CEE (Nölke and Vliegenthart 2009; Tarlea and Freyberg-Inan 2018; Tarlea, 2017). Their role in shaping the supply of skills in both countries has been limited as well. We proceed and suggest that political parties in government have played a facilitator role in economic upgrading by strategically influencing the supply of sophisticated skills. Moreover, parties that have been active in steering the skill supply have tended to be catering to the advanced sectors of the economy, placed to the economic right of the political spectrum in the post-communist context (Tucker 2006). This finding is surprising particularly, because political parties have been almost absent from political economy scholarship focusing on the region. The next section presents the methodology followed by the theoretical contribution. The fourth part presents the empirics contrasting the cases of Poland and Romania, before concluding.

1 Research puzzle and methodological approach

We are interested in the process through which political parties steered the supply of skills in these economies. The official supply of skills is closely linked to government regulation in the field of HE, but we highlight that skills are influenced from two directions: through the government investing in these skills, i.e. regulating the skills supply, and also through the influence of other institutions, such as firms and associations of firms, that invest in the skills needed by their employees.

Methodologically, we engage in a most-similar cases design (Hancké 2009) to the extent possible in an observational study. From a formal perspective, the political systems of Poland and Romania are largely similar: their bicameral parliaments are elected simultaneously and the president is directly elected. The behavioural role assumed by parties should determine policy differences, while the formal set-up of the political system should not mediate outcomes any different. Despite important institutional similarities in the two political economies, governments have played different roles in incentivizing the R&D intensity of economic activities. We trace how political parties in government regulate the production of skills while acknowledging that it would be incomplete to consider the supply of skills irrespective of demand stemming from employers.

Poland and Romania started the transition to a market economy with a large industrial sector and a strong reliance on heavy industry.[5] Foreign direct investment (FDI) flows have increased spectacularly, and MNCs have come to dominate investments and to be essential employers in the private sector (Eurostat 2017).[6] This has led researchers to characterize them as DMEs (Nölke and Vliegenthart 2009; Tarlea and Freyberg-Inan 2018). In such economies dominated by FDI, the incentives of individuals and businesses to invest in skills tend to be complementary. This equilibrium is established and maintained by the interaction of key institutions in this political economy, including universities.

Many factors need to be corroborated in order for economic sophistication to increase. As a matter of fact, Rodrik (2003) identifies three key determinants of economic growth: geography, integration and institutions. Geography and integration are largely similar in the two countries. Integration refers to market size and to the possibility to participate in international trade. We acknowledge some inherent differences between these political economies. Historically, Poland has had a stronger legacy of industrialization than Romania even though both countries had a large agricultural sector at the beginning of transition. At the same time, the geographic proximity to the high-skills economies of Germany or the Czech Republic could have facilitated the process of economic sophistication and upgrading in Poland. Nonetheless, this rather small difference in geographical position becomes negligible for the services sector, where higher value-added activities tend to concentrate. In the services sector, the duration of flights is what differences in geography boil down to. We therefore contend that for the purposes of our comparison, geographical position can be considered to be largely similar. We thus expect differences in institutions to explain the diverging outcomes in economic sophistication because they have been shown to be truly causal for economic growth (Acemoglu, Johnson and Robinson 2000).

Our analysis starts with the institutions hypothesized to have the most influence on the sophistication level of economic activities. We show step by step why several of them have not mattered in improving the economic sophistication of the DMEs of Poland and Romania. We find that governments can change incentives of essential institutions to invest in high skills even though the process is not straightforward. We note that preferences and incentives of political parties and MNCs tend to be implicit. When political parties respond to their constituency in pursuing a policy, they are likely to present the policy as universally beneficial for the entire electorate. Therefore, liberal political parties on the economic right are not expected to argue that some voters need to pay higher taxes that will be used for investments in education that will attract foreign companies to the country. Similarly, national-conservative political parties will not publicly acknowledge that they will not endorse investments in HE because they prefer direct cash transfers to the less well-off voters. Voters paying higher taxes will most likely not be the same as those benefitting from employment in these companies; hence, parties will present targeted reforms as strategic investments. Similarly, companies taking relocation decisions are expected to publicly present this as an investment for both the company and the destination country. MNCs are not expected to show public interest in lower skills or low research-intensive economies.

A good way to approximate the calculations of firms is to rely on data from sources that can reasonably be assumed to be available to these companies. This includes publicly available studies carried out by risk consulting or management consulting companies (such as PricewaterhouseCoopers or Roland Berger). Also, international organizations and international financial institutions produce publicly available studies.[7] Parties' strategies are analyzed by looking at their enacted policies.

2 Theoretical contribution and existing literature

Political economists have duly been interested to explain "how institutions evolve" (Mahoney and Thelen 2009). Change taking place in established political economies in which institutions reinforce existing equilibria is surprising. In contrast, in CEE after 1989 institutions have been redesigned with unprecedented force and scope, which makes the explanation of change appear superfluous. The fall of the communist regimes in the region meant that a multitude of paths became available (Bandelj 2008). This critical juncture (Pierson 2004) meant that, almost ironically, political parties in government continued to play a similarly decisive role as they did during the planned economy. The major difference was now determined by how parties decided to use this role. Differences between Romania and Poland have begun during these early years despite similar starting points in 1989. Broad trajectories of economic coordination were established at the beginning of the 1990s at the same time as MNCs started to enter these economies. The skills supply needs to be understood in this context.

However, the changes taking place in CEE cannot all be drawn back to the general liberalization of these markets combined with the inherited communist legacy. The variation in the sophistication level of economic activities reached by 2015 cannot be fully explained by the liberalization processes – largely similar – nor by the different starting points in the transition, as the trends in sophistication have diverged quite remarkably starting with the 1990s. Firms have been shown to be the drivers of institutional change in advanced political economies, such as France (Hancké 2002: 189). However, this argument has less explanatory power if large firms do not have strong ties to the domestic economy, as has been shown to be the case in CEE (Tarlea and Freyberg-Inan, 2018). These economies have increasingly become entrenched in the global economy, and they have come to be dominated by MNCs as employers in productive services and as sources of capital (Nölke and Vliegenthart 2009).

It is in this context that scholarly engagement with R&D in the post-communist market economies has been rather limited (but for the valuable output of Radosevic 2009). We depart in our analysis from literature that argues that the demand for low skills of firms that are active domestically determine a low quality of instruction and research in HE (Tarlea and Freyberg-Inan 2018). The demand for sophisticated labour tends to be relatively low in both private and public firms, both domestic and foreign-owned. However, the large, more productive firms tend to be MNCs (EBRD – World Bank 2017). Given that MNCs active in CEE tend to demand unsophisticated skills, students enrolled in university do not have incentives to invest in acquiring difficult-to-get skills. By having these two sets of actors – MNCs and students – following their interests, the outcome is a low-skills equilibrium where relatively low-value-added activities are carried out by a relatively low-skilled labour force (Finegold and Soskice [1988] introduced this concept). These equilibria are self-perpetuating because "once established, patterns of political mobilizations, the institutional rules of the game, and even citizens' basic ways of thinking about the political world will often generate self-reinforcing dynamics" (Pierson 2004: 10).

Strong complementarities have emerged between institutions involved in the production of goods and services, which are unlikely to be disrupted by private companies. We therefore turn to the role of political parties. Limited research so far has disentangled the influence of political parties in fostering the change of these institutions. Against the generally accepted perception of a laissez-faire ideology and a general liberalization of these markets, the role of political parties in government responding or targeting a specific constituency when deciding on policies, has been documented sporadically (Lewis 2004). Frye (2010) focuses on the importance of polarization of the political systems in the entire post-communist space in Europe and Asia, arguing that the more polarized a political system is, the less likely market-oriented reforms leading to economic growth are expected to be. Paul Lewis (2006) analyzes the important link of the institutionalization of the party system to democratization. Grzymala-Busse (2003) explains that in contexts in which one party dominates the political competition, this allows the party to extract resources from state firms or privatization deals. This leads to a larger and weaker state in which political parties use the state as a source of private rents. This has not been the case in Poland, Grzymala-Busse (2003) argues, because several parties contested (and won) elections after 1989. This has been different in Romania, where the political system has been dominated by the former communist party, the Social Democratic Party (PDSR). We further trace whether political parties representing different interests on different ends of the economic left-right spectrum (Tucker 2006) can be linked to an increase in the sophistication of economic activities.

However, the influence of political parties in government on the economy has to be distinguished analytically from state politicization, including the politicization of civil servants. State politicization, which also entails the political control of senior bureaucrats, is the equivalent of political parties in power exerting political influence on the bureaucracy. This is often associated with weak institutional development and is associated with corrupt practices. Hence, the politicization of the state can be a hindrance to development. State politicization has been a mode of governing the post-communist state (Meyer-Sahling and Veen 2012). But there has been variation in the extent to which the state has been politicized in the region. Estonia has had the lowest level of politicization amongst the new European Union member states from CEE. Here, even top ministerial positions have been found not to have been appointed politically. Slovakia and Poland, on the other hand, have had higher degrees of politicization of the bureaucracy CEE (Meyer-Sahling and Veen 2012). Romania and Bulgaria were not included in the analysis. We further move on to explaining the process through which governments can facilitate a move from low- to higher value-added activities.

2.1 Moving from low- to high-skills equilibria

The process by which economic actors – firms and workers – move from low- to relatively-high-value added activities in global value chains is referred to as economic upgrading (Gereffi 2014: 171). Poland and Romania have adopted an export-oriented model of development and became part of existing global value chains in the process of transformation into market economies. Rather than building supply chains from scratch, these countries joined existing ones. Within-industry differences are increasingly relevant in this process given that firms active in the same industry can require different levels of skills, depending on which part of the supply chain they become active in (Gereffi 2014: 19).[8] Hence, the supply of skills in the economy becomes crucial in such circumstances, determining how high up the supply chain can be joined. The more sophisticated the skills made available by the government, the higher up the supply chain can be joined. Also, the strongest link in the supply chain tends to determine the level of sophistication of the entire economy. The strongest link has tended to be represented by MNCs in both Poland and Romania, which points towards the high level of interconnection of these economies with the global economy. Moreover, these countries have been characterized as DMEs, used largely as assembly platforms by MNCs. Hence, the demand of skill sophistication for such activities has been relatively low. Ultimately, when these countries joined these global value chains, MNCs have usually intermediated the process.

Furthermore, international organizations have also played a role. The processes through which they have influenced domestic developments, also pertaining to the sophistication level of activities, have been complex. This was attempted by international organizations attaching conditions to funding or by imposing membership conditions; the World Bank or the International Monetary Fund have played such roles (Pop-Eleches 2008). More proactively, the European Union has been an instrumental actor in upgrading processes in CEE. The European Union has provided a plausible institutional model and this has been critical for the success of some Eastern European countries, such as Hungary, the Czech Republic and Poland (Hughes, Sasse and Gordon 2004). Bruszt and McDermott (2009) explain how the European Union has been essential in the reform of specific industries, especially the agricultural sector and the related food industry. In the same vein, Dobbins (2011) focuses on the positive effects of Europeanization in HE. These international institutions, particularly the European Union, can directly influence the supply of skills by imposing conditions on how many university degrees should be offered. Nevertheless, it is not clear why the European Union should have a stronger influence on the sophistication level of some member countries but less on others. We contain that this international influence has been mediated by domestic factors, which has made European policies more effective in some countries than in others. Supportive of this argument, Vachudova (2008: 861) acknowledges that political parties only respond to European Union requirements as long as this does not affect the domestic sources of their power.

Another compelling explanation for why some countries have moved up in the global value chain focuses on distinct historical legacies that should have played out differently in the two countries. The structure of the communist economy was shown to be essential for outcomes (e.g. Bohle and Greskovits 2006, 2007, 2012; Feldmann 2006; Stark and Bruszt 1998). McDermott (2002) provides a fine explanation of how the networks between firms continued to exist after the fall of communism and how these have co-determined change. It should therefore not be surprising that outcomes in Poland and Romania have diverged during post-communism if these political economies have historically been different from one another. Nevertheless, these legacies need to be absorbed and translated into policies by political parties. Historical legacies on their own do not produce policy changes, actors with agency do. Political parties in government can be the actors transforming these historical legacies, and they have done so particularly regarding the supply of HE degrees. The empirics analyzed further in the following section reveal that Polish governments have used the historical advantage in aviation due to some targeted government policies, and this has been the case in Romania as well, but to a very limited extent.

In this picture of overall low equilibrium in the region, the sophistication level of the Polish economy has increased. We analyze through process-tracing how political parties have designed policies aimed at allowing firms to upgrade the level of sophistication of economic activities conducted locally and what role the supply of skills has played in the process. Some Polish governments have helped smooth the transition from education to the labour market, thus incentivizing the different actors to invest in higher skills and activities. We find that these governments have actively contributed to shaping policies conducive to more sophisticated activities, which was largely not the case in Romania. Understanding the processes through which some economies move from vicious to virtuous cycles, i.e. increase their level of sophistication defined as percentage of R&D in economic activities, provides scholars with the opportunity to explain institutional change.

3 Empirical analysis: the supply of skills in Romania and Poland

3.1 Romania

3.1.1 Historical start of marketization

The role of the Romanian government in facilitating cooperation between HE institutions and MNCs has been limited after 1990. In the beginning of the transition, the first government in power, the successor party of the communist party (PDSR), was a promoter of a more autarkic developmental strategy. Indeed, Romania's transition to a market economy was more troubled than Poland's despite having started the transition with no foreign debt and with budget surpluses (Ban 2016). While radical reforms were pursued in Poland at the beginning of transition (Piatkowski 2013), this path was not taken in Romania. This meant privatization of state-owned companies or their modernization started later; only once the liberal centre-right alliance, Cheia, succeeded to power in 1996. This had a strong influence on the institutionalization of the market economy and on the supply of skills in the country.

Once having opened up to FDI, the government has done so unselectively. Generous direct transfers were made to citizens and to state-owned enterprises in the first years of transition to generate electoral support by the national-conservative party, the PDSR (De Menil 2003). This allowed governments to eschew longer-term oriented policies, such as higher spending on education along with an increased supply of university level skills. This lack of support for the creation of human capital is captured by the level of spending on HE. This has sustained the decreasing level of sophistication of economic activities taking place domestically.

These early policies marked differences between Romania and Poland going further. Microeconomic restructuring measures, such as the reforms of state-owned enterprises, only started after 1997. Such restructuring measures were not popular with large shares of the electorate, mostly dependent on state employment. The benefits of these reforms were not felt immediately. This also led to the defeat the centre-right alliance, Cheia, after the 2000 elections. The share of the electorate that acknowledged the potential benefits of this micro-economic restructuring that would eventually lead to the pursuit of higher-value-added activities was too small. The centre-right alliance left office after 4 years. The result was that the PDSR was in power for 11 out of the first 15 years of transition. Another aspect that made reforms more difficult than in Poland was that stakeholders in the reform process learnt how to fight their interests once having understood the rules of the game (De Menil 2003). Thus, an opportunity for radical reform immediately after the fall of communism was lost. We further consider the institutions involved in the skill formation process able to change the incentives of actors to invest in higher value-added activities.

3.1.2 Multinational companies and foreign chambers of commerce

We analyze the institutions potentially able to influence the skills supply. *Chambers of commerce* are important stakeholders in the process. These have lobbied successive laissez-faire governments in Romania in order to keep the existing framework or to ameliorate it marginally. The American and the German chambers of commerce have been active in lobbying the government for various facilities. However, their aim has not been to invest in human capital or in skills that would allow people to engage in more sophisticated activities. The American Chamber of Commerce (2014) expected "a stable, predictable, legislative and fiscal framework, coherent public policies, transparency in the decision-making process, clear country and sector strategies". These expectations are unsurprising but do not imply an upskilling of the population. If governments solely satisfy these criteria, this is unlikely to lead to an increase in the sophistication level of economic activities carried out domestically. Indeed, a survey conducted in 2013 in Romania shows that less than half of the CEOs see innovation in services and products as an opportunity to grow (PwC 2014). This speaks to the different strategies of growth MNCs have in Romania compared to Poland, as shown further as follows. Cost reduction, rather than a move up the value chain, is considered the main method of restructuring here. Businesses do not expect the government to invest in providing a highly skilled workforce. This is not surprising given the high self-selection of businesses with an interest in activities other than R&D: Only 35 per cent of CEOs in Romania believe that creating a highly skilled workforce should be one of the top three priorities of the government. This is lower than in other countries of the region. "Only 12 per cent of CEOs in Romania believe that developing an ecosystem of innovation fostering growth should be a government priority" (PwC 2014). This shows that MNCs are unlikely to incentivize governments to supply sophisticated skills, such as those needed for R&D.

But *MNCs* are the lead firms in most economic sectors (EBRD – World Bank 2017), and they tend to be the most productive private employers in the region.[9] However, few MNCs have developed strong ties locally. The ability of these companies to easily move in and out of the destination economy provides an indication of this rather weak tie of MNCs to the Romanian economy. A service centre of the ING Bank located in Cluj has moved to Hungary in 2012. Closing the service sector took place "amid economic and legislative changes in recent years that have considerably reduced its medium-term planned efficiency" (Xprimm 2014). In manufacturing, Coca-Cola, Nestle and Kraft have relocated to Bulgaria (Medrega 2013). The decision to relocate is therefore not unlikely for MNCs, and thus their incentives to invest in skills are rather limited. Despite moving abroad, some companies stay close to the border in order to be able to place products there. If a government in a DME restricts its activity to responding to the existing skills demand of companies, this demand is unlikely to emerge. Therefore, the incentives for upgrading the skills supply are unlikely to stem from these institutions.

3.1.3 Governments facilitating cooperation

The Romanian political scene has been dominated by one main party since the fall of communism, the PDSR, which has essentially remained in power after the communist regime collapsed (*Der Spiegel* 1987). The state was more freely politicized (Gryzmala-Busse 2003), which has made some authors to talk about state capture (Hellman 1998). An alternation in power took place in 1996 and again in 2004, when centre-right governments came to power.

Equally, governments headed by the PDSR have not interfered in order to change incentives of key institutions to invest in sophisticated activities. Governments headed by the liberal parties took some specific steps aimed at mediating skill formation, but the policies were not consistent throughout, as shown further as follows. Some options were available, such as attracting FDI selectively. Governments usually delegate this role to an agency for foreign investment. However, the formal institutional framework put in place by the social democratic government for promoting foreign investment after 2000 was fragile. A Romanian agency for the promotion of foreign investment (Agenția Română pentru Investiții Străine [ARIS]) stopped working in 2009 after having been put in place in 2002. This agency was headed by several managers unknown to the business environment (Medrega 2013). This happened under the centre-right government headed by Prime Minister Emil Boc. Political parties on the left and on the right had an ambivalent relationship with the business environment, and their effect on promoting higher value-added activities was severely limited. Thus, the marginal role that could have been played by political parties was rather negligible.

Nevertheless, there has been scope for cooperation between MNCs and HE institutions initiated by centre-right parties at the local level. Local authorities incentivized universities to cooperate with MNCs. In Sibiu, the engineering department of the university Lucian Blaga cooperates with tire company Continental in order to train engineers that would work at Continental (Tarlea and Freyberg-Inan 2018). Such an example emphasizes how investments in higher value-added activities in a MNC require at least some cooperation of the government with the university to train the needed employees. Hence, the supply of skills has to be assured locally. Nonetheless, such cooperation has been only sporadically mediated in Romania. Such cooperation has taken place in Romania, too, which has led to an increase in economic sophistication at a rather small scale. This gives us the opportunity to observe the counterfactual to non-cooperation of the government with universities and MNCs. Similar small-scale cooperation has taken place elsewhere in the country, in Cluj-Napoca or in Bucharest, where the government has facilitated cooperation (Medrega 2013). But these instances have not been generalized over time and space in order to lead to an increase in R&D at country level.

We notice in the Romanian case that once all institutions follow their self-interest, this leads to a perpetuation of a low-skills equilibrium. If non-governmental institutions, lead firms (MNCs), citizens themselves as well as the government fulfil their short-term goals, this keeps a low equilibrium afloat, including the supply and demand for skills. This has led to a decrease in the sophistication level of the Romanian economy, measured as R&D, while the Polish economy has registered increases, supported by targeted government policies.

3.2 The supply of skills in Poland

3.2.1 Historical start of marketization

The low-skills equilibrium in Romania has been documented in the literature, and it does not seem particularly surprising once the links between actors that keep this equilibrium afloat are understood (Tarlea and Freyberg-Inan 2018). But one question remained unsettled: *Can such an equilibrium be broken?* How has Poland, which inherited a relatively similar political-economic system, managed to escape this low-skills equilibrium? Poland has been the only European Union country not to have fallen into recession during the global economic crisis that started in 2008. Moreover, foreign capital continued to flow into Poland despite the recession and the decreasing trend of inward FDI in the region.[10] Notwithstanding, the level of sophistication of goods and services produced in the two countries has diverged, which is captured by the R&D spending levels as a percentage of GDP by private and public entities. Looking at Poland 25 years into the transition shows that historical path dependencies are not entirely deterministic.

Unlike in Romania, there has been political consensus regarding economic reform in the country immediately following the fall of communism. Polish political parties all supported the economic reform plan suggested by the International Monetary Fund (IMF) and the World Bank already at the beginning of transition (Markowski 1997: 223; Mikulova 2014). The outcome of the critical juncture produced by the regime change was therefore different to Romania. Poland opened its economy early, and it imposed harder budget constraints, which determined productivity gains (De Menil 2003). The first post-communist governments had a more important role to play than subsequent ones (Sznajder-Lee 2011). The beginning of transition has been unquestionably relevant for the general path of this political economy, because early draws in each trial have a powerful effect on the possible equilibria that will emerge (Pierson 2004).

3.2.2 Multinational companies and foreign chambers of commerce

We use the same design in our analysis, as in the case of Romania, and focus on the views of companies regarding Poland's business environment. The perspective of businesses on the economy is important for their likelihood to incentivize employees to invest in skills, and thus increasing the supply of skills in the economy. Equally, firms can also expect government support and investment in sophisticated activities.

Poland is equally strongly dependent on foreign capital. Eighty-three per cent of the 212,000 people in services in Poland work in a foreign company, according to a survey conducted by the Association of Business Service Leaders (2016). In 2016, companies considered the availability of highly skilled employees in Poland to be relatively satisfactory. Similarly, collaboration with local universities was also satisfactory, similar to the collaboration with local authorities (Association of Business Service Leaders 2016). This suggests that, similar to Romania, companies are also unlikely to have higher demands from Polish governments in terms of skills needed in R&D. Therefore, incentives for high skills do not stem from business associations or from MNCs here either. Foreign employers originating from the United States, the Nordic countries, France, the UK and Germany dominate most Polish regions, including Krakow, Wroclaw and Warsaw. Polish employers are more numerous in Lublin and Rzeszow, being prevalent particularly among IT companies (Association of Business Service Leaders 2016).

3.2.3 Governments facilitating cooperation

In Poland, political parties have been more closely monitored and regulated because no party has been able to monopolize the state (Grzymala-Busse 2003). One strategy adopted by the Polish government, the Democratic Left Alliance in 2003, was to incentivize the diversification of industrial production. Special economic zones were developed in 2003 aimed to attract foreign investment through tax incentives. Governments have fostered collaborations between businesses and universities. One such priority industry was the business services sector. The special economic zones provide tax incentives of between 25 and 50 per cent. As a result, Poland has become the largest producer of LCD sets and household appliances in the European Union (Amadeus Database 2015).

Between 2007 and 2015, the Civic Platform, generally supported by former voters of the centre-left Democratic Left Alliance and representative of the middle and upper middle classes, was in power. They also aimed to incentivize relevant actors to invest in more difficult-to-get skills. However, the mechanisms surrounding these developments have not always worked smoothly. Poland's Civic Platform government, via its education ministry, decided to offer scholarships to students studying certain subjects, namely, hard sciences. The outcome was that some students enrolled in the first year for the purpose of receiving the scholarship and quit the programme after one year. Various mechanisms can be effective when governments mediate between HE institutions and MNCs, but intentions do not always yield the expected results. Our analysis reveals that if the government assures the simultaneity of measures by, at the same time, incentivizing students, HE institutions and firms, the chances of higher value-added activities to emerge in the private sector are higher.

Indeed, the rise of the level of R&D in Poland has not been guaranteed during the transition years. Levels of R&D spending in 2000 were lower than in Romania. Moreover, a 2014 Organisation for International Cooperation and Development (OECD) report emphasizes the large disparities between the skilled and unskilled workers in the country, which provides a more realistic picture of the Polish political economy. Nonetheless, Polish governments have used two main paths for promoting R&D intensive activities: first, they have sought innovative companies by setting up special economic zones in the proximity of not only Warsaw and Krakow but also further east close to the Ukrainian border. Second, they have used foreign promotion agencies in order to attract companies working in sectors with higher levels of R&D.

As a consequence, some European banks have moved their back-office activities to Poland (Foy 2015). Firms active in the financial industry in Wroclaw and Krakow developed business solution centres, including areas in IT and HR (Goclowski and Wojciech 2015). Wroclaw Agglomeration Development Agency has been supporting both investments and tailored education programs in the Wroclaw area (ARAW 2018). Similarly, the aviation industry is advertised by the Polish investment agency to be strongly connected to the global industry and as one of the most innovative industries in the economy (Polish Investment and Trade Agency 2014). Polish companies seem to be active higher up in the value chain of this industry. The aviation valley, close to the Ukrainian and Romanian border, has attracted several companies, amongst which Hamilton Sundstrand and Hispano-Suiza (Wassik 2016). Successive governments have supported the aviation industry. The National Centre for Research and Development (NCBiR) invested €75 million between 2013 and 2017 in scientific research and in knowledge transfer to the aviation industry. The centre provides funding from both Polish sources as well as European Union funding (Aviation Valley 2017). The European Union can thus provide institutional and financial support for such measures. However, European Union funding needs to be obtained by the national government and managed through government agencies. European Union funding thus plays a similar role to historical legacies that need the agency of a government as well.

The Polish aviation industry builds on pre-existing advantages; the military has been the major historical driver of the industry. However, once the shift to a market economy was made, existing skills and existing production facilities became obsolete for the new requirements. But the Civic Platform right-oriented government simultaneously attracted capital and supplied relevant skills. The university in Rzeszow offers degrees in demand in the companies settling in the aviation valley (Rank 2014). In order for such a centre to be effective, several institutions need to cooperate. The government intervened by setting up the special economic zone and by providing university degrees in demand in the area. As a consequence of this government intervention, companies register large expenditures on R&D. They participate in international projects aimed at developing their human potential in research clusters (Bialic-Davendra and Pavelková 2014). The Krakow Technology Park was also designated as a special economic zone with a lower tax regime. Many companies are active here, including Amway, Google, IBM, Lufthansa and Tesco. Business consulting companies recommend Krakow as a top destination for outsourcing in emerging economies (Roland Berger 2010).

Nevertheless, the special economic zones are not uncontroversial in Poland's politics. The Razem ("together") Party, established in 2015 by young radical, left-oriented members, is indicative of this. They critique the special economic zones for benefitting from state-funded subsidies and tax reliefs (Majewska 2015). This hints towards the subtle and complex electoral question that governments supportive of such upgrading support need to respond to. It shows that by getting involved in such activities, they tend to do so in order to respond to their constituencies while, at the same time, losing other potential voters. Such intervention of the government in the economy will partially influence its likeliness to be re-elected. The Civic Platform was replaced in power by the Law and Justice Party (PiS) in 2015. Some legislative changes following this shift have been controversial (Spence 2016) but the special economic zones have not been affected.

This analysis shows how governments can facilitate cooperation in order to steer the supply of university-level skills. Governments responding to voters potentially benefitting from employment in the advanced sectors of the economy have made the first move by providing human capital and tax incentives. MNCs decided to engage in sophisticated activities only once a well-trained labour force existed in the economy that would sustain production activities. But governments needed to provide human capital in the first place because firms were less likely to invest otherwise given their short- and medium-term goal orientation. Similarly, institutional change in skill formation is unlikely to be determined by firms alone. But we should further contextualize our comparison within the region before moving to conclusions. We briefly mention some relevant dynamics in Estonia.

4 A regional perspective: governments and the economy in Estonia

Estonia stands out in a regional perspective as an economy that has been able to upgrade its goods and services in the post-communist period and that has relied highly on technology for service provision. It has been characterized as a liberal market economy (Feldmann 2006) with a market-based coordination of economic relations. This means that the role of the state apparatus and, hence, of the government in power is expected to be lower in comparison to other countries of the region. However, the government has played a significant role in the process despite its largely market-driven political economy. Political agency has been relevant and governments have provided the institutional framework that would allow firms to upgrade economically.

We provide a perspective on the entire economy, because the interest lies in explaining how chain and functional upgrading processes take place, i.e. the processes through which firms within countries move towards higher value-added industries requiring a higher skill content. The role of the government in facilitating this upgrading process is the more surprising, given the country's long-known inclination towards neoliberal policies. By 2014, Estonia had become the home of Skype, of health record digitalization and of internet voting, with 80 per cent internet access coverage to support the government.

Indeed, Estonia has long been a devotee of the neoliberal paradigm. Bohle and Greskovits (2012: 96) recount the role of the state in liberalizing its industries. Most importantly, Estonian governments have openly advertised the economic freedom of their country with a 0 per cent corporate income tax on all reinvested earnings. It privatized quickly and has opened up to foreign capital while registering significant economic growth.

The most surprising fact regarding the role of government in Estonia is that successive Estonian governments have played an active role in upgrading, which is at least partially unexpected for the most liberal country of the former communist bloc. Between 2004 and 2014, a centre-right party, the Estonian Reform Party (Eesti Reformierakond), has been in power. The party supported 0 per cent corporate tax and a flat income tax rate. The party tended to be supported predominantly by young, well-educated, urban voters. At least partially surprising, these liberal economic policies have been used by the government in supporting the upgrading process. At the beginning of the transition, Martin Laar, the first post-communist prime minister in power, who also served as prime minister between 1999 and 2002, was very active in promoting Estonia internationally. Estonian governments tried to project the country as a Nordic, rather than a Baltic, country. Estonia has now become by the preferred destination for Finnish and Swedish investors even though it started the transition as an underdeveloped satellite with a peripheral role in the USSR. The largest company in Estonia in 2014 was Ericsson Eesti AS, a 100 per cent Swedish company producing communication equipment. The company has grown gradually and continuously from 2004 and had an operating revenue of €1.2 million in 2014 (Amadeus Database 2015). However, Estonia had privileged initial conditions: it had more economic experimentation and more light industry than other countries in the region. Early economic reformers were able to build on this. In 1999 the Estonian president encouraged Estonian entrepreneurs and scientists in research universities to build a second Nokia, emulating their Finnish neighbours and role models (Tomusk 2003).

Tomusk (2003) describes Estonian HE to be composed of a small elitist part and a larger social sciences and humanities component that provides education at a so-called mass-level. Successive governments have had an unconcealed political will to foster the development of a technologically advanced society. Estonia has tried to preserve its tradition in the hard sciences, which contrasted to developments in Romania and Poland until 2005, where the hard sciences have not received much attention. According to the WEF's 2012–2013 Global Competitiveness Index, Estonia was ranked highest in CEE for the quality of its math and science education. About one-third of Estonians have obtained a HE degree and more than half of the adult population speaks at least one foreign language. The young tend to speak English and the older population Russian (Estonian Investment Agency 2014).

The government has reformed the legal system in order to support entrepreneurship so that foreign investors are treated equally as locals when intending to establish companies. A significant proportion of the state budget has been spent for supporting entrepreneurs. "We found that the match between the skills, and also the culture fit, was very great. And on top of that, the passion for IT in Estonia convinced us that this is really the place we have to go", chief information officer Martin Kolbe explained in an interview (Estonian Investment Agency 2014).

The stated concern of successive Estonian governments to improve its competitiveness and to attract investment is visible at the level of the government agency meant to promote foreign investment. The clear website of the government agency also includes a talent map showing the national and regional "talent pools" in some key areas: engineering, technical IT, foreign languages, financial services and environmental technologies. They offer skills assessments as well. So, the government has been powerfully active in the reform of these sectors. The comparison of Poland and Romani to Estonia is by design imperfect: modernizing a country of 1.3 million people should be easier than one that is 20 or 40 times larger and that has traditionally relied on heavy industry base and has large populations of non-productive peasant farmers (*The Economist* 2013).

Moreover, Balaji (2017) points out that interpreting the Estonian success story should be tempered: "Estonia's main problem at the moment is not to make it 'easier for start-ups to attract foreign talent' but to find a way to prevent its own citizens from abandoning the country in ever-greater numbers". This is not a surprising occurrence in the region where the out-migration of highly skilled individuals is well documented (Warrell 2018). This also shows that coordinating reforms needs to respond to a series of incentives that are difficult to be influenced by the government on its own. But it comes to show that even in an economy traditionally relying on market forces, the role of the government cannot be underestimated.

Nonetheless, the Estonian IT bubble is not uncontested despite the strong support it receives from the government. "Remember the .com bubble? The .ee bubble is next" is the title of a blog post in which professionals in the industry criticize the support of the state for both foreign and domestic IT companies (.ee Bubble 2016). At the same time, Estonia is considered a good collaborator for Indian companies to work with in the IT sector (Balaji 2017). This is a clear indication that a focus on a given industry, particularly if the state is involved, implies redistributive measures, which tend to create losers and winners.

This wider perspective on the region seems to emphasize that governments can, and do have, an obvious impact on the development of the economy, and they do cater to their constituencies when deciding on policies. Even in economies that are largely market-driven, such as the liberal market economy of Estonia, the role of the government in creating collaboration and incentives for upgrading cannot be underestimated.

Conclusion

Political parties in government after the fall of communism have designed the new political-economic institutions of the region. They continue to regulate policies and to influence the skill supply through HE institutions. However, scholarly engagement aimed at explaining the variation in governments' role in such public policies in the post-communist democracies has been surprisingly narrow. This chapter aims to fill this gap by explaining the link of political parties to the skills supply and to economic governance in the post-communist context.

We explain institutional change in skill formation in these new democracies by showing how governments have mediated relationships between employers and employees. While doing so, we zoomed in on three strategies of governments that have been associated with an increase in the level of economic sophistication: bargaining with MNCs, incentivizing students to invest in skills relevant for upgrading and creating HE degrees relevant for specific needs of companies. We highlighted how these policies have allowed firms active in the two countries to become part of value chains at different levels of economic sophistication.

Moreover, political parties in government that have acted as mediators between institutions of skill formation leading to the pursuit of higher value-added activities have tended to respond to different constituencies than parties that have not been active in this role. This was the case in Poland and Romania alike. Political parties catering to voters employable in the advanced sectors of the economy, such as the Civic Platform in Poland, have been designing policies that increased the supply of sophisticated skills. Parties catering to voters that have not capitalized on the new economic conditions in the market economy, such as the PDSR in Romania, have not played this mediating role. Thus, the space for manoeuvre of the government in the area of skill formation has been exploited differently by parties, and this can be linked back to the constituencies of these parties.

The chapter acknowledges the interdependencies between firms and institutions of skill formation. Strong institutional complementarities are conducive to low equilibria – low skills and low sophistication. Therefore, many factors need to be corroborated in order for economic activities to move from low- to higher-skills equilibria and governments can be instrumental in this process. They can provide incentives towards coordination at higher levels of instruction and production.

As these countries become more engaged in developing higher-value-added services, competition for FDI between the governments of CEE will become even more acute. This may pose even more challenges to the countries that are now trapped in low-skills equilibria. The chapter suggests that political parties should figure more prominently in political economy scholarship focusing on CEE. Moreover, this work speaks to a broader debate about the role of political parties in skill formation and in institutional change more generally.

Notes

1 The International Standard Classification of Education (ISCED) is widely used in comparative studies (Eurostat 2016).

2 We define R&D expenditures according to World Development Indicators 2017 (World Bank 2017). Expenditures for research and development are current and capital expenditures (*both public and private*) on creative work undertaken systematically to increase knowledge, including knowledge of humanity, culture and society and the use of knowledge for new applications. R&D covers basic research, applied research and experimental development.

3 Researchers in R&D are professionals engaged in the conception or creation of new knowledge, products, processes, methods or systems and in the management of the projects concerned. Postgraduate PhD students (ISCED-97 level 6) engaged in R&D are included.

4 We use *upgrading* and *moving from low- to high-skills equilibria* interchangeably in the text. This is further explained in the literature section.

5 Industry value added as a percentage of GDP was 36 per cent in Romania and 38 per cent in Poland in 1995. This changed to 34 per cent in Poland and 35 per cent in Romania. Industry comprises value added in mining, manufacturing, construction, electricity, water and gas (World Bank 2017).

6 Twenty-five per cent of the employees in the private business employment were working in MNCs in 2010 in Romania and 15 per cent in Poland (Eurostat 2017).

7 This includes the World Bank (WB) or the International Monetary Fund (IMF), the Organisation for International Cooperation and Development (OECD) and reports by the relevant Directorates-General (DGs) of the EU Commission.

8 Literature differentiates between different types of upgrading. Product upgrading implies moving into more sophisticated product lines, process upgrading requires a more efficient input-output relation and superior technology. Functional upgrading means acquiring functions to increase the overall skill content of the activities. Chain upgrading implies moving to new but oftentimes related industries.

9 Structural Business Statistics, comparing value-added at factor cost of private employers with foreign affiliated statistics (FATS; Eurostat 2014).

10 FDI rose by 38 per cent in 2011 compared to 2010 according to data from the National Bank of Poland.

References

Acemoglu, D., Johnson, S. and Robinson, J.A. (2001) "The colonial origins of comparative development: An empirical investigation". *American Economic Review*, 91 (5): 1369–1401.

Agencja Rozwoju Aglomeracji Wrocławskiej (ARAW) (2018) *Wroclaw Agglomeration Development Agency*. Available at: www.araw.pl (Accessed: 13 September 2018).

Amadeus Database (2015) Available at: https://www.bvdinfo.com/en-apac/our-products/economic-and-m-a/m-a-data/zephyr (Accessed: 13 September 2018).

American Chamber of Commerce (2014) *Invest in Romania!* Ebooklet. Available at: https://www.amcham.ro/index.html/articles?articleID=1819 (Accessed: 13 September 2018).

Association of Business Service Leaders (2016) *Business service sector in Poland*. Available at: www.absl.pl (Accessed: 2 November 2017).

Aviation Valley (2017) *Official webpage of the Polish Aviation Valley*. Available at: www.dolinalotnicza.pl/en/about-us/ (Accessed: 8 February 2017).

Balaji, S. (2017) "Why Estonia may be the best place for India's overlooked startups to flourish", *Forbes*, May 26. Available at: www.forbes.com/sites/outofasia/2017/05/26/why-estonia-may-be-the-best-place-for-indias-overlooked-startups-to-flourish/#4a5b1183196c (Accessed: 20 June 2018).

Ban, C. (2016) *Ruling ideas: How global neoliberalism goes local*. Oxford: Oxford University Press.

Bandelj, N. (2008) *From communists to foreign capitalists: The social foundations of foreign direct investment in postsocialist Europe*. Princeton, NJ: Princeton University Press.

Bialic-Davendra, M.L. and Pavelková, D. (2014) *The clusters phenomenon in the selected central European countries*. Cambridge: Cambridge Scholars Publishing.

Bohle, D. and Greskovits, B. (2006) "Capitalism without compromise: Strong business and weak labor in Eastern Europe's new transnational industries", *Studies in Comparative International Development*, 41(1): 3–25.

Bohle, D. and Greskovits, B. (2007) "Neoliberalism, embedded neoliberalism and neocorporatism: Towards transnational capitalism in Central-Eastern Europe". *West European Politics*, 30(3): 443–466.

Bohle, D. and Greskovits, B. (2012) *Capitalist diversity on Europe's periphery*. Ithaca, NY: Cornell University Press.

Boix, C. (1997) "Political parties and the supply side of the economy: The provision of physical and human capital in advanced economies, 1960–1990", *American Journal of Political Science, 41(3)*: 814–845.

Bruszt, L. and Greskovits, B. (2009) "Transnationalization, social integration, and capitalist diversity in the East and the South", *Studies in Comparative International Development*, 44(4): 411–434.

Bruszt, L. and McDermott, G.A. (2009) *Transnational integration regimes as development programmes*. New York: Springer.

Busemeyer, M.R. (2015) *Skills and inequality: The political economy of education and training reforms in Western welfare states*. Cambridge: Cambridge University Press.

De Menil, G. (2003) *In search of prosperity: Analytic narratives on economic growth*. Princeton, NJ: Princeton University Press.

Dobbins, M. (2011) *Higher education policies in Central and Eastern Europe: Convergence towards a common model?* Basingstoke: Palgrave Macmillan.

EBRD – World Bank (2017) *Business environment and enterprise performance survey (BEEPS)*. Available at: www.ebrd.com/pages/research/economics/data/beeps.shtml (Accessed: 20 January 2018).

The Economist (2013) How did Estonia become a leader in technology? Available at: www.economist.com/the-economist-explains/2013/07/30/how-did-estonia-become-a-leader-in-technology (Accessed: 30 August 2018).

.ee Bubble (2016) ".ee Bubble Receives Funding from Enterprise Estonia". .ee Bubble. Available at: http://doteebubble.blogspot.com/ (Accessed: 20 June 2018).

Estonian Investment Agency (2014) "New Estonian-located development teams of foreign enterprises". Available at: https://investinestonia.com/new-estonian-located-development-teams-of-foreign-enterprises/ (Accessed: 13 September 2018).

Eurostat (2016) "Statistical approaches to the measurement of skills 2016 edition", Statistical Working Papers. Available at: http://ec.europa.eu/eurostat/documents/3888793/7753369/KS-TC-16-023-EN-N.pdf/438b69b5-2fcb-4923-b9e2-fa7b59906438 (Accessed: 13 September 2018).

Eurostat (2017) *Foreign affiliates statistics*. Available at: https://ec.europa.eu/eurostat/web/structural-business-statistics/global-value-chains/foreign-affiliates?p_p_id=NavTreeportletprod_WAR_NavTreeportletprod_INSTANCE_MlPTx882pcau&p_p_lifecycle=0&p_p_state=normal&p_p_mode=view&p_p_col_id=column-2&p_p_col_pos=1&p_p_col_count=3 (Accessed: 30 August 2018).

Feldmann, M. (2006) "Emerging varieties of capitalism in transition countries: Industrial relations and wage bargaining in Estonia and Slovenia", *Comparative Political Studies*, 39(7): 829–854.

Finegold, D. and Soskice, D. (1988) "The failure of training in Britain: analysis and prescription", *Oxford Review of Economic Policy*, 4(3): 21–53.

Foy, H. (2015) "Poland draws big banks for 'nearsourcing'", *Financial Times*. Available at: www.ft.com/content/1df9e49c-a153-11e4-8d19-00144feab7de (Accessed: 13 March 2018).

Frye, T. (2010) *Building states and markets after communism: The perils of polarized democracy*. New York: Cambridge University Press.

Gereffi, G. (2014) "Global value chains in a post-Washington consensus world", *Review of International Political Economy*, 21(1): 9–37.

Goclowski, M. and Wojciech, Z. (2015) "Swiss banks trade Zurich's costly charm for Polish provinces', *Reuters*. Available at: www.reuters.com/article/us-swiss-snb-banks-offshoring/swiss-banks-trade-zurichs-costly-charm-for-polish-provinces-idUSKBN0LJ0BD20150215 (Accessed: 13 September 2018).

Grzymala-Busse, A. (2003) "Political competition and the politicization of the state in East Central Europe", *Comparative Political Studies*, 36(10): 1123–1147.

Hall, P.A. (1986) *Governing the economy: The politics of state intervention in Britain and France*. Oxford: Oxford University Press.

Hancké, B. (2002) *Large firms and institutional change: Industrial renewal and economic restructuring in France*. Oxford: Oxford University Press.

Hancké, B. (2009) *Intelligent research design: A guide for beginning researchers in the social sciences*. Oxford: Oxford University Press.

Hellman, J.S. (1998) "Winners take all: The politics of partial reform in post-communist transitions", *World Politics*, 50(2): 203–234.

Hughes, J., Sasse, G. and Gordon, C. (2004) "Conditionality and compliance in the EU's eastward enlargement: Regional policy and the reform of sub-national government", *Journal of Common Market Studies*, 42(3): 523–551.

Jensen, C. (2011) "Capitalist systems, deindustrialization, and the politics of public education", *Comparative Political Studies*, 44(4): 412–435.

Lewis, P. (2006) "Party systems in postcommunist Central Europe: Patterns of stability and consolidation", *Democratization*, 13(4): 562–583.

Lewis, P.G. (2004) "Political parties and the representation of social interests in Central Europe". In ECPR joint session, Workshop paper. Available at: https://ecpr.eu/Filestore/PaperProposal/e34f8082-9ad3-47b8-a033-573707c95a1e.pdf (Accessed: 30 August 2018).

Mahoney, J. and Thelen, K. (eds.) (2009) *Explaining institutional change: Ambiguity, agency, and power*. Cambridge: Cambridge University Press.

Majewska, E. (2015) "Together – another politics is possible: The Razem Party in Poland and hope for the new", *Lefteast*. Available at: www.criticatac.ro/lefteast/together-another-politics-is-possible-the-razem-party-in-poland-and-hope-for-the-new/ (Accessed: 3 January 2017).

Markowski, R. (1997) "Political parties and ideological spaces in East Central Europe. Communist and post-communist studies", *Communist and Post-Communist Studies*, 30(3): 221–254.

Markowski, R. and Tucker, J. "Euroscepticism and the emergence of political parties in Poland", *Party Politics*, 16(4): 523–548.

McDermott, G.A. (2002) *Embedded politics: Industrial networks and institutional change in postcommunism*. University of Michigan Press.

Medrega, C. (2013) "Dupa desfiintarea ARIS, investitiile straine in Romania au fost in cadere libera. Ce este de facut", *Ziarul Financiar*, September 6. Available at: www.zf.ro/eveniment/dupa-desfiintarea-aris-investitiile-straine-au-fost-in-cadere-libera-ce-este-de-facut-11296528 (Accessed: 13 September 2018).

Meyer-Sahling, J.H. and Veen, T. (2012) "Governing the post-communist state: Government alternation and senior civil service politicisation in Central and Eastern Europe", *East European Politics, 28*(1): 4–22.

Mikulova, K. (2014) "'Potemkin Europeanisation'? Dynamics of party competition in Poland and Hungary in 1998–2004", *East European Politics and Societies*, 28(1): 163–186.

Nölke, A. and Vliegenthart, A. (2009) "Enlarging the varieties of capitalism: The emergence of dependent market economies in East Central Europe", *World Politics*, 61(4): 670–702.

Piatkowski, M. (2013) "'Poland's new golden age': Shifting from Europe's periphery to its center", World Bank Policy Research Working Paper, (6639).

Pierson, P. (2004) *Politics in time: History, institutions, and social analysis*. Princeton, NJ: Princeton University Press.

Polish Investment and Trade Agency (2014) "How to do business in Poland". Available at: www.paiz.gov.pl/publications/how_to_do_business_in_poland (Accessed: 3 December 2016).

Pop-Eleches, G. (2008) *From economic crisis to reform: IMF programs in Latin America and Eastern Europe*. Princeton, NJ: Princeton University Press.

PricewaterhouseCoopers (PwC) (2014) *PwC CEO survey*. Bucharest: PricewaterhouseCoopers Romania.

Radosevic, S. (2009) "Research and development, competitiveness and European integration of South Eastern Europe", *Europe-Asia Studies*, 61(4): 621–650.

Rank, S. (2014) "Insight – Polish aviation industry seeks Australian connections, Aviation Business". Available at: www.austrade.gov.au/australian/export/exportma

rkets/countries/poland/news/insight-polish-aviation-industry-seeks-australian-connections (Accessed: 20 January 2017).

Roberts, A. (2009) *The quality of democracy in Eastern Europe: Public preferences and policy reforms*. Cambridge: Cambridge University Press.

Rodrik, D. (1996) "Understanding economic policy reform", *Journal of Economic Literature*, 34(1): 9–41.

Rodrik, D. (2003) *In search of prosperity: Analytic narratives on economic growth*. Princeton, NJ: Princeton University Press.

Roland Berger Strategy Consultants, Preveden, V., Sturm, M. and Koppendorfer, M. (2010) "Cee in 2020: Trends and perspectives for the next decade". Available at: http://blog.iese.edu/bizknowledgewatch/2011/cee-in-2020-%E2%80%93-trends-and-perspectives-for-the-next-decade/ (Accessed: 30 August 2018).

Spence, A. (2016) "Orban's media playbook, now coming to Poland", *Politico*. Available at: www.politico.eu/article/orban-media-playbook-coming-to-poland-media-law-human-rights-european-values/ (Accessed: 8 January 2016).

Der Spiegel (1987) "Rumänien: Kluger Kopf", *Spiegel Online*. Available at: www.spiegel.de/spiegel/print/d-13525483.html (Accessed: 15 March 2018).

Stark, D. and Bruszt, L. (1998) *Postsocialist pathways: Transforming politics and property in East Central Europe*. Cambridge: Cambridge University Press.

Sznajder-Lee, A. (2011) "After the party, the after-parties? The effects of communist successor parties on economic reform in Central and Eastern Europe", *Europe-Asia Studies*, 63(9): 1697–1718.

Tarlea, S. (2015) *Dependency and development in Central and Eastern Europe's new capitalist systems* (Doctoral dissertation, University of Oxford).

Tarlea, S. (2017) "Higher education governance in Central and Eastern Europe: A perspective on Hungary and Poland", *European Educational Research Journal*, 16 (5): 670–683.

Tarlea, S. (2018) "Low- and high-skills equilibria in Central and Eastern Europe: What role for the government?" *East European Politics and Societies and Cultures*: 0888325418777059.

Tarlea, S. and Freyberg-Inan, A. (2018) "The education skills trap in a dependent market economy: Romania's case in the 2000s", *Communist and Post-Communist Studies*, 51(1): 49–61.

Tomusk, V. (2003) "Aristoscientists, academic proletariat and reassembling the megamachine: 21st century survival strategies of the estonian academia", *International Studies in Sociology of Education*, 13(1): 77–100.

Tucker, J.A. (2006) *Regional economic voting: Russia, Poland, Hungary, Slovakia, and the Czech Republic, 1990–1999*. Cambridge: Cambridge University Press.

UNESCO (2017) *UNESCO Institute for Statistics 2017*. Available at: http://uis.unesco.org/ (Accessed 30 August 2018).

Vachudova, M. (2008) "Tempered by the EU? Political parties and party systems before and after accession", *Journal of European Public Policy*, 15(6): 861–879.

Warrell, H. (2018) "'Eastern European migration to the UK in 5 charts' New ONS analysis on migrants from EU 8 countries including Poland and Hungary", *Financial Times*. Available at: www.ft.com/content/14b558c8-6585-11e7-8526-7b38dcaef614 (Accessed: 26 June 2018).

Wassik, Z. (2016) "Aviation Valley becomes an engine of growth for Poland", *Financial Times*. Available at: www.ft.com/content/ff4b32ce-90a9-11e6-a72e-b428cb934b78, (Accessed: 25 January 2017).

World Bank (2017) *World development indicators 2017*. Available at: https://data.worldbank.org/products/wdi (Accessed 13 September 2018).

World Economic Forum (WEF) (2012) "Global competitiveness report 2012/2013", technical report, Geneva: World Economic Forum.

Xprimm (2014) "ING Group closes down the regional service center in Cluj", *Xprimm*. Available at: www.xprimm.md/ING-Group-closes-down-the-regional-service-center-in-Cluj–inaugurated-six-months-ago-articol-197,198,200-30814.htm (Accessed: 15 March 2018).

Conclusion

The book explains under what conditions some countries upgrade economically while others do not. This concern has preoccupied scholars of political economy and policy makers for years and will continue to figure prominently in scholarly work and in policy circles. Despite broadly similar economic and higher education (HE) policies, the Central and Eastern Europe (CEE) countries have diverged from one another and, most importantly, have not caught up with the core Organisation for International Cooperation and Development (OECD) countries.

We approached this research question with an empirical focus on CEE. First, we explained why the CEE countries have come to function at a relatively low skills equilibrium after becoming democracies and market economies. We argued that the relatively low equilibrium in production and training is a consequence of the developmental strategy embraced by the governments in the region – the unconditioned reliance on foreign capital, specifically on multinational companies (MNCs) and the intentional lack of investment in education. Second, we explained how and why some countries have eschewed this low-skills equilibrium. Governments in countries which have upgraded their economic activities have done so by attracting MNCs to carry out more sophisticated activities requiring a higher level of skills. Governments in these countries bargained with MNCs to attract higher value-added activities and simultaneously incentivized students to invest in skills. This has contributed to improving their HE systems. These questions were approached by developing a theoretical argument and by providing empirical support for it in individual chapters.

Separate chapters analyzed the extent to which each institution can partly explain the variation in HE policies and in the sophistication level of economic activities developed by firms that are active domestically. The broad research question is split into several finer-grained ones in individual chapters. The chapters provide further explanations on how HE policies and the sophistication level of economies are linked. Chapter 1 showed how the Romanian education system sustains the status of the Romanian political economy as a dependent market economy. Chapter 2 asked to which extent the strong position of MNCs explains the low investment in skills by students and by universities. Chapter 3 argued that the emergence of different levels of sophistication of these economies can be explained by the divergent actions of governments regarding upgrading. Chapter 4 showed how the Hungarian and the Polish HE systems are linked to their political economies.

The core argument brought forward is that the key to understanding variation in HE dynamics in the region is by accounting for the role of governments and of employers in jointly determining HE policies. Moreover, this can be best understood by relying on a model developed as a new variety of capitalism, the dependent market economy (DME). The DME model was previously defined by Nölke and Vliegenthart (2009) and is used in this book as a (partly redefined) tool for explaining processes of skill formation in these transition economies. MNCs are a key employer for highly educated people. Largely, MNCs do not need particularly high skills in CEE, which keeps these economies entrenched in a low-skills equilibrium. Some governments seem to understand these dynamics and to be able to tackle them by steering their economies on upward trajectories, inter-alia, by investing more in HE.

The book thus explains the causes and consequences of HE dynamics in a historical institutionalist context. This contribution is timely and relevant because it provides a new avenue for understanding the complex mechanisms of HE governance. At the same time, the book sheds new light on the role of transnational capital and its influence on skill formation in the region and on economic development more broadly.

This is the first extensive research on the political-economic determinants of HE that focuses on the new democracies in CEE, and even in a larger context, in developing market economies. The expertise on the evolution of skill formation in the region before the start of this research was extremely limited. Hence, this exercise is almost by definition incomplete, being the first such study on skill formation in the region. Despite inherent limitations, the contribution of the book is theoretical, empirical and methodological.

Chapters 1 and 2 entail an implied comparison of the CEE countries with their hypothetical more developed counterparts – such as the rest of the OECD. This is a comparison of economic sophistication and skills development in CEE with the alternative developmental trajectory as predicted by the most optimistic observers of the transition period (as summarized by Campos and Coricelli 2002). As Slater and Ziblatt (2013), convincingly argue, every research enterprise is necessarily comparative. Relying on counterfactuals in the analyses in Chapter 1 and Chapter 2 required an analytical exercise. This was achieved by asking what would have happened if governments invested more in HE and MNCs would have required higher skills. Equally, what would have happened if MNCs left these countries is another potential avenue considered in the second chapter. Chapters 3 and 4 provide a comparison of the various countries within the region. The shifting comparative perspective between the former two and the latter two chapters provided fertile ground for empirical and theoretical exercises. They allowed to explore the variation in HE development in a relatively homogenous set of countries, as further detailed in the following sections.

Chapter 1

Chapter 1 contributes to the book in several ways. First, while Romania is an interesting empirical case, observing HE in that country provided an opportunity to disentangle the role of skill formation in a less successful political economy. The case study of Romania was the least likely case for a DME and the most likely case for an economy characterized by a low-skills equilibrium. The chapter highlights the role of the demand for skills in determining the quality of HE. It explains how, despite the fact that any actor would be better off if more resources would be invested in skill formation, there are no real incentives for any of the actors to invest in better skills unilaterally. This low-skills equilibrium is defined in line with the work of Finegold and Soskice (1988). The chapter draws a bleak picture of a low-skills equilibrium DME; it shows the relationships that emerge between MNCs, governments and HE institutions. It argues that it is extremely difficult to change the reinforcing dynamics between institutions. It dwells deep into the types of relationships that emerge between actors and it shows how they are interlinked.

Second, the chapter is also an important cornerstone of the book, because it provides insights into the incentives and preferences of a set of stakeholders – employers and academics, employees in NGOs, students – on the basis of interviews. How do students adapt to the perceived opportunities in the labour markets? How do managers of HE institutions and those of MNCs think of one another? What are the types of skills they provide and demand, respectively? The interviews revealed that each of the actors adapts to the envisioned strategies of the other actors. The interviews also suggested that actors rationalize but that their information is not always complete. This is the reason why students decided to invest in certain types of degrees while also working simultaneously. This comprehensive analysis of stakeholders provides some confidence that the hypotheses formulated in the case study and further analyzed in the book account for a wealth of alternative explanations. The case study of Romania uses an inductive approach and it provides the ideal setting to formulate hypotheses. It does so in a necessarily explorative setting. However, it would have been impossible to achieve such broad coverage otherwise. Not all of the hypotheses advanced in Chapter 1 proved to have been correct. The most interesting turn the book takes in the following chapters regards the determining role of political parties for the low-skills equilibrium. While political parties in government seem unable to change this equilibrium to a higher level in Romania, the following chapters prove that this is a possibility.

Third, it provides an ideal setting for defining concepts to be used in the book. Most important of all, HE quality, while rightly defined by education specialists as complex (Harvey and Green 1993), can be proxied for the large-n analyses by the indicator of funding/enrolment. This insight is used when moving from within to across case analyses and from qualitative to quantitative approaches. Relying on these indicators allows to test for the generality of the findings.

Fourth, a prerequisite for analytical narratives, such as those provided in Chapters 3 and 4, was the detailed description of processes largely unknown in political science literature, such as the evolution of HE, which are provided in Chapter 1. All in all, Chapter 1 provides hypotheses and exploratory insights into the political-economic determinants of HE in a low-skills equilibrium DME. Moreover, it also shows that the actors involved in the interactions are relatively well-informed regarding the other actors' preferences.

Chapter 2

Chapter 2 provides some empirical tests of the implications of the DME by analyzing the hypothesized relationships within a larger quantifiable framework. While micro foundations should ideally be explored for every set of actors hypothesized as relevant, Chapter 2 analyzes the micro foundations at the firm level. This is an essential validating empirical exercise, and the first such test to be conducted on the empirical implications of a political economy model in the region to date (Frye [2010] explores micro foundations in a different theoretical framework). It provides a systematic analysis of firm-level data and distinguishes between MNCs and other domestically active MNCs. This chapter thus provides better empirical grounding for the model by showing that MNCs are more likely to employ highly educated people than similar domestic companies. The chapter also presents supporting data at the country level on employment in MNCs and on the relevance of foreign direct investment (FDI) in a comparative framework.

Chapter 2 also provides a more intuitive and structured diagram of the logic of the DME model, presenting it as a game of strategic interaction. This allows it to be understood by scholars across disciplines. The interactions leading to a low-skills equilibrium are presented in a stylized, simplified way. The next chapters allow for more complexity, showing that the active role of political parties can break this vicious cycle.

Chapter 3

Chapters 3 and 4 move on to explore differences between countries in the region. Chapter 3 documents the change that has taken place, while Chapter 4 provides some explanations for the domestic drivers of this change: political parties. The most important difference in approach between the first two chapters and the last two chapters of the book is the role played by political parties.

Chapter 3 highlights differences in activity between countries at the industry level. It adds one more level of detail to the empirical analysis – the sectoral level. Differences in terms of production and in terms of skill formation are analyzed. The chapter traces more carefully the processes that have led to an increase in the sophistication level of activities in some countries but not in others. It is argued that an increase in the level of education spending is positively associated with the likelihood of countries developing higher value-added activities. In the case studies, we analyze this relationship and provide an illustration of the mechanisms that can drive the upgrading process. These analyses show that a government can have an active role in processes of upgrading from low- to high-skills equilibria and that a simultaneous increase in enrolment and in demand of highly educated people can lead to more sophisticated activities.

Chapter 4

In Chapter 4 the question naturally emerged of why some governments have been more committed to fostering economic upgrading while others have not. Or do governments invest in HE as soon as this seems likely to lead to positive consequences? More abstractly, this chapter distinguishes between the role of the agency and of the structure in determining outcomes. Electoral politics can explain the differences in HE development. Right-oriented governments have tended to be more responsive to the structure of the economy when deciding to support upgrading processes. The case studies provide focus on stories that are suggestive of the mechanisms at play.

The chapters address the research question from different angles. Given the nature of the data and of the approach, some chapters focus more on exploring differences over time as potential explanations for change, while others are centred on more static relationships. The last two chapters explore dynamics over time. The levels of analysis shifted from individual- to industry- and to country-level indicators. The two approaches adopted complemented one another as detailed in the next sections.

Research Design

One could argue that the prerequisite for theory is methodology and the prerequisite for methodology is data. Hence, the raw empirical findings are presented first, then how these findings were reached and, at last, what this entire enterprise adds to the theoretical debates in the discipline.

The empirics covered in the book had previously been to a great extent unknown to political scientists and to political economists focusing on the region and beyond. The book thus broadens the field. First, HE enrolments have increased significantly in the entire region, but the increase has been more pronounced in the social sciences than in other fields. Funding has not increased to the same extent as enrolment. Political parties on both the right and the left of the political spectrum have allowed for an increase in enrolment, but increased funding has been associated with governments dominated by parties on the right. Second, MNCs employ a larger proportion of highly educated people than similar domestic companies. MNCs tend to be more sophisticated and also larger than comparable domestic companies. They have also tended to move in and out of CEE markets with relative ease.

And third, governments dominated by parties of the right have tended to spend more on HE as a percentage of GDP than governments dominated by left-wing parties. Steering HE has tended to be responsive to the sophistication level of the economy when right-oriented parties were in power.

Other aspects that had been unknown empirically and that should be further analyzed and explored in future work are the different stances of political parties on policies towards HE. In Romania, the left-oriented social-democratic party has tended to favour increase in HE enrolment, while the right-oriented political coalitions have promoted policies to limit enrolment. These existing cleavages between political parties towards HE governance can be found in several of the CEE countries, in Poland and Hungary specifically. These interesting empirical patterns can be explored further in future work on education policies. At the same time, the question that remains is whether similar empirical patterns can be identified regarding other public policies as well.

The book combines a comprehensive case study with statistical analyses of large-N data at different levels of analysis complemented by paired comparisons. The relatively unexplored territory required a more innovative research design in order to grasp the processes of interest. Reconciling the holistic view on political economic developments of the varieties of capitalism (VoC) literature with the individualistic approach of "scientific realism" (Keohane 2009: 39) can only be partially achieved. List and Spiekermann (2013: 629) identify this divide in political science "between methodological individualists, who seek to explain political phenomena by reference to individuals and their interactions, and holists (or nonreductionists), who consider some higher-level social entities or properties such as states […] causally significant."

Increasingly, more attention is being devoted to issues related to causal inference in political science literature (following Angrist and Pischke 2008). Paying more attention to issues of causal inference is likely to allow researchers overcome some of the shortcomings of observational correlational research. Therefore, more research should be conducted going further to isolate more clearly the causal effects of institutions on public policies, particularly regarding the effect of different parties in government on public policies.

Another way to test for causal effects would be to rely on other types of data than purely observational one. Experimental data, using both surveys and field experiments can be another way to test the magnitude of the causal mechanisms proposed in the book. Once more data becomes available, more sophisticated statistical techniques can be applied as well. All these methods have their own limitations as well, but they can be used complementarily to the approaches used in this book. We focus in the following on the contributions of this book.

Substantive Contribution

Skill formation

One contribution is the analysis of skill formation processes in transition economies. In the European context, little had been known about the capacity of the CEE political economies to produce human capital. Therefore, tackling the questions and puzzles concerning HE development in CEE could rely only partially on existing academic research. Previous scholarly writings have been relied on in the book and developed further.

One valuable source has been the research of scholars of the education sciences. Voldemar Tomusk's work has been an important source for understanding processes of HE reform in the region (Tomusk 2000).[1] At the same time, numerous studies, each focusing on small areas of HE policy and governance, were relied on in an attempt to understand perceptions of HE dynamics (Galbraith 2003). We abstracted from this work and reinterpreted many of the claims in an attempt to explain the political economy of HE development. The bureaucratic apparatus of the HE system does not always function in an efficient way to transform inputs into outputs.

In a broader perspective, the entire literature on skill formation rests on the work of Gary Becker (1960) and his analyses of human capital and education. In these approaches, human capital is treated on par with physical capital. Historical institutionalists, such as Thelen (2009), identify and explain the embeddedness of training systems in the national political economic models. This book follows in these footsteps and explains how the production of skills, especially of advanced degrees, such as those offered by HE institutions, is also embedded in the national political economies of CEE. HE institutions are intertwined with the structure of the economy, similar to what Thelen identifies at the level of vocational training. Thelen (2004) explains cross-national differences in training systems by developing an argument about political coalitions that determine outcomes, and she links that to the settlements achieved in the early industrial period between three critical groups: independent artisans, skilled industrial workers and employers in skills-intensive industries. These settlements were heavily mediated by state action (or inaction), which either facilitated coordination, both amongst firms and between unions and employers, or not. In turn, this book explains how state action can facilitate coordination between institutions demanding and supplying skills in an emerging democracy and market economy.

But most importantly, we argued that HE provides an ideal entry point towards understanding broader political economic processes. This analysis of skill formation as an adequate way to explain broader political economic processes is inspired by the literature on VoC in its broadest interpretation. In this literature, (Iversen and Soskice 2001 being one example), explaining education processes facilitates the understanding of broader coordination mechanisms between institutions of skill formation, including vocational training and HE (Busemeyer and Trampusch 2012). This literature is enriched by this book by its different geographical focus, but also, most importantly, by the fact that it shows that the relationships identified between institutions in other contexts do not need to hold universally. It shows, for example, that HE enrolments and financing do not need to be correlated, as commonly assumed in political economy scholarship (Ansell 2010; Busemeyer and Iversen 2014). Moreover, the book emphasizes that HE institutions play a similar role to vocational training in a political economy but, even more important, that HE is essential for economic upgrading.

While HE is famously different from other welfare state institutions, such as pensions or unemployment, broader theoretical implications can be derived from here that can be used in analyses of other welfare policies. Political parties and MNCs are likely to have strong effects on other state policies in Central and Eastern Europe, too. Nevertheless, the incentives of individual actors vis-à-vis any of these other policies will be different, and the insights gained from analyzing HE can be transferred to other areas only cautiously. Therefore, one important lesson that can be learnt from other policy areas is the fact that individual incentives will likely influence public policies and that political parties and MNCs need to be taken into account in any analysis of policy in CEE.

Other than contributing to existing scholarship on skill formation, this research adds to literature on historical institutionalism broadly construed. It explains institutional change in a set of countries about which not much had been known.

Institutional change

The book highlights commonalities and differences amongst ten CEE countries. All these countries are dependent on FDI; initial conditions were largely similar at the beginning of transition and they have registered significant economic growth and explosive HE enrolment rates. Nonetheless, the skills produced by HE institutions in the region have diverged, and this book has attempted to explain this variation. Existing theoretical approaches seemed partly suitable but partly unsuitable to explain these developments. Therefore, theories, such as the DME model itself, were unravelled and redesigned (Nölke and Vliegenhart 2009). I have argued that mutually reinforcing relationships link education, employment and politics. It emerged from the empirics analyzed that complementarity between these institutions is sustained by the incentives of different actors that adapt to the perceived opportunities in the labour market.

Institutions are inter-related within these generally stable DMEs. Hence, change will not emerge easily given the reinforcing equilibria sustained by the different actors. The research has shown that incremental change can take place if governments have the capacity (or the will) to foster it. A configuration of factors coordinated by political parties – MNCs and HE coordinated in a predetermined direction – can lead to change and to superior (or inferior) equilibria. Moreover, political parties, do not act out of their own will but are linked to voters. Their representation function is thus essential (Whitefield and Loveless 2013, for example).

Institutional cooperation can also be a source of change. Hancké (2012) has shown that chambers of commerce can play an important role in collective skill formation by solving coordination problems. Moreover, this literature considers labour relations as causally relevant, and this should be further explored.

Individual incentives of voters can change if their socio-economic status changes, if they envision their chances in the labour market to improve and if the government in power enacts different types of policies. Therefore, this is likely to change the expectations voters form towards the party representing them. This is likely to change the behaviour of parties as well, and it is likely that the policies towards MNCs and the governance of HE will change as well. This has the potential to lead to institutional change. The mechanism leading to institutional change has been identified and explained into detail in the third and fourth chapters. Thus, this book has portrayed a world in which institutions do not exist because of the functions they fulfil, but rather as an outcome of individual incentives.

These institutional complementarities have not been perfect, either at the theoretical or at the empirical level. Another source of change in these political economies can be the mismatches at different points in time. One example of intentions and actual outcomes not coinciding has been when students opted to receive a scholarship to study technical subjects in Poland but did not end their studies, as explained in the case studies in Chapters 3 and 4.

Domestic institutions and development

The role played by MNCs in development is highly dependent on the domestic conditions in the destination countries. This is almost ironic, given that the argument of the book started by emphasizing the importance of international capital for these economies and how (unilaterally) dependent they are on this capital. But domestic institutions have the capacity to determine outcomes. Hence, the book argued for bringing the state back in (Schmidt 2009) by highlighting the role of political parties in government for economic development. A case study of Romania in Chapter 1 has shown that political parties have played a marginal role in determining change but this is not the case by default. All in all, this book argues that integrating research on the political composition of governments can shed a new light on the developmental premises of these economies.

The role of political parties and their influence on HE policy and upgrading are theorized in this book (Busemeyer and Trampusch 2011; Estevez-Abe, Iversen and Soskice 2001). Significant and extremely valuable work had previously been conducted on the emerging political systems in the region (Grzymala-Busse 2002; Pop-Eleches 2008; Tavits and Letki 2009). However, scholars have not given political parties and HE as much credit as they are given here. This book described a different causal mechanism, linking political parties to economic growth. The relevance of political parties in economic development can certainly be explored in future research.

Future research

Alternative explanations for the puzzles identified in the research can be considered in future work. First, the role of the European Union and of migration in these economies should be further explored. Parties in government can facilitate upgrading through the influence they have on HE and on MNCs. However, the European Union can be a facilitator of change as well, as Bruszt and McDermott (2012) and Hughes, Sasse and Gordon (2004) have shown. The process of European integration is likely to determine governments to adapt their strategies and to foster upgrading. The expectation is that this will affect governments equally, but this can be tested empirically.

Second, the level of integration with the EU, which is strongly correlated with the distance from Brussels, also plays a role in the capacity of these economies to upgrade. Bohle and Greskovits (2012) refer to CEE as a "periphery", implying a geographical distance from a centre. It would therefore be sensible to test the validity of some spatial econometrics models when attempting to explain why some countries have been more successful than others in devoting resources to HE. The level of integration with the European Union can be measured as the time, since countries have been European Union members or members of the Eurozone.

Third, one should look into the preferences of voters with regards to HE funding and enrolment and whether and how this is mediated by the employment status and the income level of voters (Gingrich and Ansell [2012] focus on OECD data). A fifth aspect that has been bracketed out is the impeding role played by corruption. Political parties may not represent their voters as unequivocally as assumed here, as argued by Mares and Petrova (2014).

All in all, this is a contribution to development literature concerning how some countries manage to improve their economies while others do not. Using the case of CEE, the book draws broader theoretical conclusions about countries leaving state-centred models and move towards market-oriented economies. It presents a theory concerning dependent development and countries attempting to catch up. It contributes to debates in political economy and comparative politics by analyzing the role of MNCs, of HE and, equally relevant, of political parties in economic development. It shows mechanisms and relationships that have the potential to explain other contexts. Therefore, the scope-conditions of the theory can be broadened to refer to the transition from totalitarian regimes in North Africa, Central Asia or Eastern Europe.[2]

The analysis of the countries of CEE has can help us explain processes taking place outside of this context. When thinking about how the lessons drawn from here can be transposed, this should be done with caution. An interesting insight gained from the book should be the careful analysis of individual incentives determining processes of skill formation. This is a valid exercise that should be conducted more generally. Therefore, questions about incentives structures should be asked with reference to other contexts in both the field of skill formation as well as more generally regarding public policies.

The book advances a new analytical narrative about HE in the region. This is the first contribution in political economy in CEE focusing on the role of human capital formation. This contribution takes the role of political parties seriously in new democracies and market economies. Moreover, if political parties in government pursue different policies regarding HE, this is expected to influence other sectors as well. If the resources of the government are limited, then one expectation is that political parties will also have different effects on other sectors, such as defence or health care as these are redistributive policies.

This contribution should inform policy-makers as well. While much discussion in the policy area has been devoted to input indicators on HE reform in transition economies, one bold implication of this book is that reforming HE cannot be achieved by only targeting HE. The way in which incentives work at the individual level requires a coordinated effort of employers and employees to improve HE. In other words, if the government decides to improve HE and the (potential) students do not find reasons to invest in HE, this will not suffice for HE to improve. We cannot expect the HE sector to outperform the economy given the complementarities between HE and other sectors of the economy.

Notes

1 Tomusk was the director of the Education Department at the Open Society Foundation, based in London since the beginning of transition until 2010.

2 Transition economies in Central Asia and Eastern Europe are listed in order of the magnitude of their FDI flows in 2012 (UNCTAD, World Investment Report, 2013): Russia, Kazakhstan, Ukraine, Turkmenistan, Azerbaijan, Belarus, Croatia, Uzbekistan, Albania, Georgia, Bosnia and Herzegovina, Montenegro, Armenia, Kyrgyzstan, Serbia, Tajikistan, Republic of Moldova and Macedonia.

References

Angrist, J.D. and Pischke, J.S. (2008) *Mostly harmless econometrics: An empiricist's companion*. Princeton, NJ: Princeton University Press.

Ansell, B. (2010) *From the ballot to the blackboard: The redistributive political economy of education*. Cambridge: Cambridge University Press.

Becker, G.S. (1960) "Underinvestment in college education?" *The American Economic Review*, 50(2): 346–354.

Bohle, D. and Greskovits, B. (2012) *Capitalist diversity on Europe's periphery*. Ithaca, NY: Cornell University Press.

Bruszt, L. and McDermott, G.A. (2012) "Integrating rule takers: Transnational integration regimes shaping institutional change in emerging market democracies", *Review of International Political Economy*, 19(5): 742–778.

Busemeyer, M.R. and Iversen, T. (2014) "The politics of opting out: explaining educational financing and popular support for public spending", *Socio-Economic Review*, 12(2): 299–328.

Busemeyer, M.R. and Trampusch, C. (2011) "Review article: Comparative political science and the study of education", *British Journal of Political Science*, 41(2): 413–443.

Campos, N.F. and Coricelli, F. (2002) "Growth in transition: What we know, what we don't, and what we should", *Journal of Economic Literature*: 793–836.

Estevez-Abe, M., Iversen, T., and Soskice, D. (2001) "Social protection and the formation of skills: a reinterpretation of the welfare state", in Hall, P.A. and Soskice, D. (eds.), *Varieties of Capitalism: The Institutional Foundations of Comparative Advantage*: 145–183. Oxford: Oxford University Press.

Finegold, D. and Soskice, D. (1988) "The failure of training in Britain: Analysis and prescription", *Oxford Review of Economic Policy*, 4(3): 21–54.

Frye, T. (2010) *Building states and markets after communism: The perils of polarized democracy*. Cambridge: Cambridge University Press.

Galbraith, K. (2003) "Towards quality private higher education in Central and Eastern Europe", *Higher Education in Europe*, 28(4): 539–558.

Gingrich, J. and Ansell, B. (2012) "Preferences in context micro preferences, macro contexts, and the demand for social policy", *Comparative Political Studies*, 45(12): 1624–1654.

Grzymala-Busse, A.M. (2002) *Redeeming the communist past: The regeneration of communist parties in East Central Europe*. New York: Cambridge University Press.

Hancké, B. (2012) *Multinational companies and the production of collective goods in Central and Eastern Europe*: 295–308. Cheltenham: Edward Elgar Publishing.

Harvey, L. and Green, D. (1993) "Dening quality", *Assessment and Evaluation in Higher Education*, 18(1): 9–34.

Hughes, J., Sasse, G., and Gordon, C. (2004) "Conditionality and compliance in the EU's eastward enlargement: Regional policy and the reform of sub-national government", *Journal of Common Market Studies*, 42(3): 523–551.

Iversen, T. and Soskice, D. (2001) "An asset theory of social policy preferences", *American Political Science Review*, 95(4): 875–894.
Keohane, R.O. (2009) "The old IPE and the new", *Review of International Political Economy*, 16(1): 34–46.
List, C. and Spiekermann, K. (2013) "Methodological individualism and holism in political science: A reconciliation", *American Political Science Review*, 107(4): 629–643.
Mares, I. and Petrova, T. (2014) *Patronage and intimidation: The use of the state in elections in contemporary Eastern European elections.* Manuscript, Columbia University.
Nölke, A. and Vliegenthart, A. (2009) Enlarging the varieties of capitalism: The emergence of dependent market economies in East Central Europe", *World Politics, 61*(4): 670–702.
Pop-Eleches, G. (2008) *From economic crisis to reform: IMF programs in Latin America and Eastern Europe.* Princeton, NJ: Princeton University Press.
Schmidt, V.A. (2009) "Putting the political back into political economy by bringing the state back in yet again", *World Politics*, 61(3): 516–546.
Slater, D. and Ziblatt, D. (2013) "The enduring indispensability of the controlled comparison", *Comparative Political Studies*, 46(10): 1301–1327.
Tavits, M. and Letki, N. (2009) "When left is right: Party ideology and policy in post-communist Europe", *American Political Science Review*, 103(4): 555–569.
Thelen, K. (2004) *How institutions evolve: The political economy of skills in Germany, Britain, the United States, and Japan*. Cambridge: Cambridge University Press.
Thelen, K. (2009) "Institutional change in advanced political economies", *British Journal of Industrial Relations*, 47(3): 471–498.
Tomusk, V. (2000) "When east meets west: decontextualizing the quality of East European higher education", *Quality in Higher Education*, 6(3): 175–185.
UNCTAD, G.V.C. (2013) "Investment and trade for development", in *World investment report*. Geneva: UNCTAD.
Whitefield, S. and Loveless, M. (2013) "Social inequality and social conflict: Evidence from the new market democracies of Central and Eastern Europe", *Europe-Asia Studies*, 61(1): 26–44.

Index